GERMAN FLAK DEFENCES
VS
ALLIED HEAVY BOMBERS

1942–45

DONALD NIJBOER

OSPREY PUBLISHING
Bloomsbury Publishing Plc
PO Box 883, Oxford, OX1 9PL, UK
1385 Broadway, 5th Floor, New York, NY 10018, USA
E-mail: info@ospreypublishing.com
www.ospreypublishing.com

OSPREY is a trademark of Osprey Publishing Lt d

First published in Great Britain in 2019

A catalogue record for this book is available from the British Library.

ISBN: PB 9781472836717; eBook 9781472836724; ePDF 9781472836700;
XML 9781472836731

19 20 21 22 10 9 8 7 6 5 4 3 2 1

Edited by Tony Holmes
Cover artwork and battlescene by Gareth Hector
Aircraft and armament profiles and three-views and Engaging the Enemy
artwork by Jim Laurier
Maps and formation diagrams by www.bounford.com
Index by Zoe Ross
Typeset by PDQ Digital Media Solutions, Bungay, UK
Printed in China by Toppan Leefung Printing Ltd.

Osprey Publishing supports the Woodland Trust, the UK's leading woodland
conservation charity.

To find out more about our authors and books visit **www.ospreypublishing.com**.
Here you will find extracts, author interviews, details of forthcoming events and
the option to sign up for our newsletter.

Acknowledgements

I would like to thank my partner Janet, Jon Lake, Jonathan Falconer, Robert
Forsyth, Uwe Jack and Edward Westermann for their advice and assistance in
completing this book.

B-24D Liberator cover art

On 9 October 1942 24 B-24Ds from the 93rd BG made the group's combat
debut over the European continent. It was also the first time the Eighth Air
Force had despatched more than 100 bombers (24 B-24s and 108 B-17s) on a
mission. The five-group raid targeted the steel and engineering works and
locomotive and freight car plant in the French city of Lille. Flying Fortresses
from the 92nd, 97th and 301st BGs led the way, with the Liberators falling in
behind. Over the target, the B-24s were optically targeted by the flak defences
and hit by accurate fire. B-24D 41-23722 *BOMERANG* of the 93rd BG's
328th BS received the most attention, with the bomber being nursed back to
its Alconbury, Cambridgeshire, base by 1Lt John Stewart. Once the aircraft
was back on the ground, crew chief MSgt Charles A. Chambers could not
believe the condition 'his bomber' was in – more than 200 holes were counted
in the fuselage and wings. *BOMERANG* was duly classified as economically
unrepairable because of the high degree of damage it had suffered, the bomber
being deemed fit for spare parts reclamation only. Both Stewart and Chambers
successfully argued for a reprieve, however, with 41-23722 being repaired and
returned to flying status. *BOMERANG* would go on to survive the carnage of
the Ploesti raid on 1 August 1943 to become the first B-24 to complete
50 missions in the European Theatre of Operations. After 53 missions, the
veteran bomber was flown back to the USA and sent on a war bond tour.

Flak tower cover art

RAF Bomber Command's main campaign against the city of Berlin would last
from 20 August 1943 until 25 March 1944, with 19 raids being mounted
during this period. At the heart of Berlin's flak defences were three massive flak
towers, each of which was armed with four twin-barrelled 128mm guns
(capable of firing a formidable 60 rounds per minute) and numerous 20mm
and/or 37mm cannon. One of the first bunkers built (*Gefechtsturm I*) was
located in the Tiergarten at the Berlin Zoo, with two more following in the
Friedrichshain and Humboldthain districts. On the night of 24/25 March
1944, Bomber Command launched its last and costliest raid against the
German capital. Of the 811 bombers despatched (577 Lancasters,
216 Halifaxes and 18 Mosquitoes), 72 were shot down. The majority of the
aircraft lost fell to flak – 44 Lancasters and 28 Halifaxes. The Battle of Berlin
would cost the RAF no fewer than 607 heavy bombers – 421 Lancasters,
151 Halifaxes and 35 Stirlings. (Both cover artworks by Gareth Hector)

Previous Page

For protection against low-level air attacks, German heavy flak towers were
equipped with 20mm and 37mm weapons. The most numerous was the
20mm Flakvierling 38 automatic cannon, seen here, which grouped four such
weapons onto a single gun mounting. (Author's Collection)

CONTENTS

INTRODUCTION

'Flak damaged many aircraft and drove the bombers to fly high, but it destroyed few.'
Max Hastings, author of *Bomber Command*

In myriad publications chronicling the air war between the Allied heavy bomber force (both RAF and USAAF) and the Luftwaffe, the role and effectiveness of Germany's ground-based gun defences (heavy, medium and light) has largely been ignored. The vast majority of Anglo-American histories have focused mainly on the role of the Luftwaffe's fighters (both during daylight operations and at night), with little or no mention of the immense contribution made by the thousands of flak batteries and searchlights based both in occupied Europe and Germany itself.

Adolf Hitler's rise to power in 1933 triggered a new European arms race. Well aware of Germany's vulnerability to air attack, Hitler believed strongly in a robust ground-based air defence and fighter interceptor force. The result was the rapid expansion and acquisition of flak guns in the six years leading up to World War II.

The British, also well aware of the potential and the effects of aerial attack, made their own plans. During World War I, British civilians had been subjected to aerial attack by both German Zeppelins and Gotha twin-engined bombers flying from airfields in occupied Europe. Between May–July 1917 alone, Gotha bomber attacks on London and the southeast of England had resulted in 322 people being killed and 852 injured. The panic these raids caused among British politicians and the Press was considerable, although they affected the civilian population far less seriously. To counter the threat, fighters were recalled from France and more anti-aircraft guns and searchlights were deployed in depth.

Immediately after the attacks, Lt Gen Jan Smuts (who was part of the Imperial British War Cabinet), with the support of British Army and Royal Flying Corps

officers, studied how the armed forces had responded to the Gotha bomber offensive in 1917. His findings, known as the Smuts Report, led directly to the creation of the Royal Air Force (RAF) as an independent service. Buried in the report, Smuts had planted the seeds of change that would eventually lead to the RAF's strategic air offensive during World War II. Captivated by the vision of air power and its future potential, Smuts wrote:

> And the day may not be far off when aerial operations, with their devastation of enemy lands and destruction of industrial and populous centres on a vast scale, may become the principal operations of war, to which the older forms of military and naval operations may become secondary and subordinate.

Smuts' vision would germinate and grow, and for the next 20 years the RAF would hone its theories surrounding long-range bombing and eventually form the world's first strategic bomber force.

In the USA, air-minded individuals like 1Lts James H. 'Jimmy' Doolittle (subsequently leader of the 'Doolittle Raid' on Tokyo in April 1942 and commander of the Twelfth, Fifteenth and Eighth Air Forces in World War II) and Henry H. 'Hap' Arnold (later to become the Chief of the Army Air Forces in 1941) also embraced and actively promoted the idea of a strong bomber force. Like their RAF counterparts, proponents of the bomber in the US Army Air Corps (USAAC) saw the aircraft as a transformative weapon of war, and one that could prove decisive in the next global conflict. The one issue that would dog both services, however, was bombing accuracy.

Bomb-aiming results during the 1930s were generally poor, and they would remain a problem throughout World War II. Heavy flak would make matters even worse for bomb aimers. While the four-engined heavy bomber continued to be at the leading edge of military technology during the conflict, its bomb load, once released, was a crude and inaccurate weapon.

One of the few colour photographs showing German flak. Taken from the tail gunner's position, this shot shows B-17Gs of the 385th BG ploughing through heavy flak en route to their target in late 1944. The white target indicators immediately above the central Flying Fortress denote a 'blind bombing' mission using H2S radar. (Author's Collection)

As the RAF and USAAC grappled with the technical problems of building and fielding an effective bombing force, the Third Reich was preparing for war on the ground and in the air. By 1935 doctrine was in place, the Luftwaffe being seen as an instrument of attack and defence by German military strategists:

> From the start of the conflict, the air forces bring the war to the enemy, while the anti-aircraft artillery directly protects the homeland. The primary mission of the anti-aircraft artillery is the defence of the homeland in cooperation with the fighter force.

The last sentence is key. Anti-aircraft defences cannot be looked at in isolation. An effective air defence requires both fighters and flak batteries. It has often been stated that it took 16,000 88mm shells to shoot down an Allied bomber. It was an example of how wasteful anti-aircraft fire was compared to a fighter attack on a formation of bombers. To say the flak gun was not as efficient at shooting down a bomber compared to a fighter misses the point. This was a false metric, and one that the Germans fell prey to during the war.

It must be remembered that the first job of the anti-aircraft gun was to make bombers fly higher, thus decreasing the accuracy of their attacks. More 'hot metal up' meant less 'cold, accurate steel coming down'. Its second job was to try and break up incoming formations, or cause them to use evasive manoeuvres. In late March 1945, Gen Carl A. 'Tooey' Spaatz, commander of US Strategic Air Forces in Europe, stated that flak was 'the biggest factor' affecting bombing accuracy. As a rough calculation, each 5,000ft increase in altitude halved the accuracy of anti-aircraft fire. However, as previously noted, the greater the bomber's height, the poorer the accuracy when it came to hitting the target. Bombing errors from 15,000ft were twice as great as from 5,000ft.

Flak had a direct effect on accuracy, but it also had some real and important hidden effects. Anti-aircraft fire damaged tens of thousands of aircraft, with Boeing B-17 Flying Fortresses and Consolidated B-24 Liberators forced out of their protective formations proving easy prey for Luftwaffe fighter pilots. Flak-damaged bombers at night, their positions exposed by fire and smoke or reduced speeds, provided marauding nightfighters with tempting targets. Flak also had a delayed effect. Most flak splinters were relatively small, resulting in nicked fuel, hydraulic or oil lines. The gradual loss of these vital fluids caused many bombers to crash-land in Axis territory or ditch in the North Sea, while numerous others would limp back to England and then have to be force-landed. Damaged bombers also required repair, reducing serviceability rates.

Flak also killed and maimed. The psychological reaction of aircrew forced to face flak and searchlights in their daily or nightly raids took their toll. Morale at times would suffer and target accuracy became an issue, with crews bombing early in order to avoid the worst of the flak.

Unfortunately for Allied aircrew, both the RAF and USAAC had focused their resources on developing bombers that could repel fighter attacks. Little or no thought was given to the danger posed by flak. Equipped with sophisticated powered turrets and flexible guns, new bombers like the Short Stirling (the RAF's first operational heavy bomber) and the B-17 were thought to be more than capable of defending

themselves against fighter attack, bombing the target and then returning home. All the turrets and extra guns only added more weight and excess drag, reducing the bombers' speed and service ceiling – both key defensive attributes. Indeed, the Stirling III's low operational ceiling of just 17,000ft left it dangerously vulnerable to flak and nightfighters, resulting in the aircraft suffering heavier losses in comparison with Bomber Command's other four-engined 'heavies', the Handley Page Halifax and Avro Lancaster. Conducting its first operational mission on the night of 10/11 February 1941, the Stirling was withdrawn from operations over Germany in mid-March 1944 due to heavy losses.

In the first year of war, the RAF's 'strategic bombing' of Germany left much to be desired. Two raids on naval ports in December 1939 had all but shattered the concept of the self-defending bomber, with 17 of 36 Wellingtons sent on these missions being shot down by flak and fighters. More losses would follow, forcing Bomber Command to embrace night-bombing as the best way to strike Germany.

America's entry into World War II following Japan's attack on Pearl Harbor on 7 December 1941 added a new dimension to the air war. By the autumn of 1942 the Third Reich now faced a two-pronged attack consisting of RAF heavy bombers by night and B-17s and B-24s of the USAAF's Eighth Air Force by day. Early attacks were limited to targets in France and the Low Countries – between 17 August and 9 October 1942, the Eighth Air Force conducted 14 missions against targets predominantly in France. While losses were minimal, bombing accuracy proved disappointing.

These raids only reinforced the concept of the self-defending bomber. According to the USAAF's official history, the bombers were 'more than able to hold their own against fighter attack, even with a minimum of aid from the escorting fighters'. These

This photograph was taken on 5 July 1941 during 'Circus 33' – the first daylight mission involving the Stirling, and the first time an Allied four-engined heavy bomber had attacked an enemy target. The Fives-Lille steel works in northern France was bombed that day, with Flt Lt Bob Gilmour's Stirling I N3658/LS-E of No. 15 Sqn (surrounded by flak bursts as the bombers crossed the French coast) being one of three such aircraft involved in the operation. This raid had a heavy fighter escort and no Stirlings were lost. Spitfires and Hurricanes could not protect the bombers from flak, however, and between 7 and 19 July three Stirlings fell to enemy gunners during daylight raids. (Author's Collection)

A US serviceman stands beside a captured 88mm FlaK 37 gun. During the war German industry produced more than 20,000 FlaK 18/36/37s, which formed the backbone of the *Flakwaffe*. Each of the four white rings on the barrel of this FlaK 37 denote an aircraft shot down by the weapon. (NARA)

early missions led group commanders to downplay the dangers of German flak and fighters, as 'at no time had they presented a serious threat to our bombers'. While some staff officers in the USAAF downplayed the threat of flak, bomber crews knew differently. Shortly after Col Curtis E. LeMay led the 305th Bombardment Group (BG) to England in the autumn of 1942, he asked his counterpart Col Frank A. Armstrong of the 97th BG his opinion about enemy flak. Armstrong answered, 'the flak is really terrific' and 'if you fly straight and level for as much as ten seconds, the enemy are bound to shoot you down'.

This was a view increasingly echoed by regular bomber aircrew too, as the aerial campaign against Germany grew in its ferocity. One such individual was B-17 waist gunner Sgt William J. Howard of the 351st BS/100th Bomb Group:

All the missions scared me to death. Whether you had fighters or not, you still had to fly through the flak. Flak was what really got you thinking, but I found a way to suck it up and go on.

For the coming battles, the Allies would pit their best heavy bombers – the Stirling, Halifax, Lancaster, B-17 and B-24 – against the Luftwaffe's formidable ground defences, which consisted of thousands of 88mm, 105mm and 128mm heavy guns and even more light and medium 20mm and 37mm flak guns. The battle would rage both day and night. For aircrew, flak would be a horrifying constant of the brutal strategic bombing campaign, often arriving unannounced and with deadly accuracy. Allied heavy bomber losses due to flak would number in the thousands. Indeed, German flak accounted for close to half of all American aircraft lost in Europe, making it a lethal and deadly adversary.

CHRONOLOGY

1928
January The Weimar Republic's *Reichswehr* Minister, Otto Gessler, resigns after news of Germany's secret rearmament programme in violation of the Treaty of Versailles is exposed. Part of that programme had seen the first Zeiss-built *Kommandogerät* P 27 fire director system enter service with the *Reichswehr*, followed shortly thereafter by the first Krupp-built FlaK L/60 75mm anti-aircraft gun.

1930
February The *Reichswehr* establishes the *Flakartillerie*.

1933
30 January Adolf Hitler is named Chancellor of Germany. He describes the nation's armed forces 'as the most important institution in the State'. Germany's rearmament begins in earnest shortly thereafter.
December The 88mm FlaK 18 heavy gun enters service. With an effective ceiling of 26,000ft, it incorporates direct transmission of firing solutions from the fire director to the gun. This significantly increases its rate of fire.

1934
8 August Formal design proposal tendered by the USAAC for a multi-engined bomber capable of supporting operations in Hawaii, Panama and Alaska.

1935
26 February Luftwaffe is officially established.
Summer By mid-year the Reich's ground defences include 15 heavy and three light flak battalions. A heavy battalion consisted of three batteries of four 88mm guns.
28 July Maiden flight of the four-engined Boeing Model 299, precursor to the B-17.

1936
Spring The British Air Ministry issues specification B.12/36 for a new four-engined heavy bomber. This request would result in the development of the Stirling and Halifax.
14 July RAF Bomber Command formed.

1937
1 March First Y1B-17 "Flying Fortress" delivered to the USAAC's 2nd BG.

An early-build B-17B seen at Boeing Field, Seattle, on 27 July 1939. A total of 39 B-models were constructed in a single production run in 1939–40, these aircraft being powered by four Wright 1,200hp R-1820-51 Cyclone engines. (Author's Collection)

Autumn	Rheinmetall-Borsig commences testing of the 128mm FlaK 40 gun.

1938

Spring	Rheinmetall-Borsig 105mm FlaK 38 heavy gun reaches production.
June	State Secretary of the *Reichsluftfahrtministerium* (RLM), General Erhard Milch, orders the creation of an Air Defence Zone stretching from Germany's border with Switzerland to the North Sea.

1939

14 May	First flight of the Short Stirling from Rochester aerodrome.
1 September	German flak forces comprise 657 heavy batteries, 560 light batteries and 188 searchlight batteries.
4 September	The RAF sends a mixed force of 15 Blenheim IVs and 14 Wellington bombers to attack the German warships. The Blenheim IVs target the heavy cruiser *Admiral Scheer* and the light cruiser *Emden* moored in Wilhelmshaven harbour, while the Wellingtons target ships in Brunsbüttel. Bomber Command duly suffers its first casualties of the war, with five Blenheim IV downed by flak and two Wellingtons falling to German fighters.
25 October	First flight of the Handley Page Halifax prototype.
29 December	Prototype Consolidated XB-24 completes first flight.

1940

25–26 August	First RAF bombing raid on Berlin, with 103 aircraft (Hampdens and Wellingtons) being dispatched. Three bombers lost to flak.

1941

9 January	First flight of Avro Lancaster prototype. Aircraft quickly reveals its superiority over the Stirling and Halifax.
10–11 March	First operational flight by the Halifax, with six aircraft from No. 35 Sqn targeting Le Havre docks.
Spring	Telefunken FuMG 39T(C) *Würzburg D* gun-laying radar enters service.
8 July	The RAF's No. 90 Sqn gives the B-17 (in Fortress I form) its combat debut when three examples bomb Wilhelmshaven.

For many RAF bomber crews, getting caught in a search light beam was their 'greatest fear'. As the war progressed, searchlight batteries played a vital role in the *Flakwaffe*'s air defence. The *Flakscheinwerfer* (Flak Searchlight) 34 and 37 used 150cm-diameter parabolic glass reflectors capable of achieving an output of 990 million candelas. (Author's Collection)

1942

12 January — *Flakwaffe* created as part of the *Flakartillerie*.

14 February — General Directive No. 5, subsequently known as the Area Bombing Directive, sent to Bomber Command by the Air Ministry, instructing it to target the German industrial workforce and the morale of the population through the systematic bombing of cities.

10 March — No. 44 Sqn undertakes first Lancaster mission over Germany.

30–31 May — RAF uses 'bomber stream' tactics during Operation *Millennium* (first 'thousand-bomber raid') on Cologne.

8 November — First raid by a mixed formation of USAAF B-17s and B-24s targets Saint-Nazaire U-boat pens.

December — By year-end 50 flak cars (armed with 20mm light flak guns) are operating in defence of the German rail network.

1943

3 January — Eighth Air Force suffers its heaviest losses to date – seven B-17s shot down, three B-24s damaged beyond repair and 44 B-17s and three B-24s damaged to varying degrees. Flak is responsible for much of this.

24–25 July — First use of *Window* to foil German radar during an RAF raid on Hamburg (part of the Battle of Hamburg).

17 August — Eighth Air Force attacks Schweinfurt and Regensburg with 361 B-17s. Sixty are lost to flak and fighters, 11 damaged beyond repair and a further 162 damaged but repairable.

17–18 August — RAF bombs the German research establishment at Peenemünde, on the Baltic coast, the site being targeted by 324 Lancasters, 218 Halifaxes and 54 Stirlings.

October — USAAF bombers introduce anti-flak radar countermeasures, employing *Carpet* and *Window* jamming methods.

2 November — USAAF's Fifteenth Air Force commences heavy bomber operations against the Third Reich from bases around Foggia, in Italy.

18 November — Air Chief Marshal Arthur 'Bomber' Harris, Commander-in-Chief (C-in-C) RAF Bomber Command, orders his crews to commence the Battle of Berlin. Eighteen more raids follow, ending on 24–25 March 1944.

1944

January — German flak defences protecting the Reich now number 1,234 heavy batteries and 693 light batteries. This is a 61 per cent increase in numbers from 1942.

20 February — Eighth and Fifteenth Air Forces launch Operation *Argument*, targeting major German aircraft and engine assembly plants.

4 March — Eighth Air Force bombers attack Berlin for the first time.

24/25 March — 811 RAF bombers attack Berlin and 44 Lancasters and 28 Halifaxes are destroyed – approximately 50 by flak, with the rest falling to nightfighters.

1945

1–19 April — Fifteenth Air Force B-24s conduct two trial attacks against German flak batteries in Italy.

25 April — Luftwaffe 128mm flak gun crews atop Berlin's flak towers trade artillery fire with Soviet Red Army units entering the city.

DESIGN AND DEVELOPMENT

'Anti-aircraft guns were plentiful, but relatively speaking, provided with poor radar control. They did not prove a very lethal weapon – even when they were most numerous.'
The Strategic Air War Against Germany 1939–45 – British Bombing Survey

ALLIED HEAVY BOMBERS

The creation of the four-engined strategic bomber was largely built on faith. Prior to the outbreak of World War II, both the RAF and USAAC held firm in their belief in the apparent future capabilities, and invincibility, of the heavy bomber as a weapon for strategic offence. Senior British and American officers envisioned fleets of well-armed, high-flying bombers using pin-point accuracy to destroy factories (crippling the enemy's armed forces) and urban centres at will. The end result of such attacks, they believed, would be panic, prompting the terrorized citizenry to demand that their government surrender. Brig Gen William M. 'Billy' Mitchell, avid bomber proponent and one-time Assistant Chief of the US Army Air Service (USAAS), summed it up best:

> The result of warfare by air will be to bring about quick decisions. Superior air power will cause such havoc, or the threat of such havoc, in the opposing country that long drawn-out campaigns will be impossible. Woe be to the nation that is weak in the air.

The delivery of American-built Martin B-10 bombers to the USAAC from November 1933 represented a huge leap forward in aeronautical technology and design. Using all-metal construction, the monoplane B-10 was equipped with retractable landing gear, a rotating front gun turret, internal bomb-bay, full engine cowlings, flaps, variable-pitch propellers and a fully enclosed glass cockpit. In a single stroke the B-10, which was capable of 213mph in level flight, made virtually all previous biplane bombers and, perhaps more significantly, fighters obsolete. For the advocates of strategic bombing, the appearance of the B-10 only reinforced their argument that massed formations of bombers, using speed, altitude and their own defensive armament, would be immune to attack.

Moving forward, designers of heavy bombers focused on increasing the range, speed, bombload and armament of their aircraft – all areas deemed to be critically important by leading air forces across the globe. Greater service ceiling, however, was ignored. RAF doctrine throughout the 1930s, for example, focused on daylight bombing from an altitude of just 10,000ft. At this height, any British bomber then in service would have been within easy reach of the 88mm FlaK 18 anti-aircraft gun. The RAF simply ignored the dangers posed by flak, convinced that speed through the flak zone was the best form of protection. This assumption was shared by the USAAC, with Capt Lawrence S. Kuter, an instructor at its Tactical School, remarking that, 'anti-aircraft fire may be annoying, but should be ignored'.

As advanced as the Martin B-10 was, it was only as good as its bombsight. The whole *raison d'être* of the heavy bomber was to get ordnance on target. Bombing results from World War I were dismal, and this had been fully appreciated at the time. Indeed, the American Expeditionary Force booklet on high-altitude bombsights, published on 20 August 1918, had plainly stated that 'in order to drop a bomb so that it will strike at least in the vicinity desired, the use of a bombsight is imperative. However, this sight must be simple enough to use it even under hostile fire.' Testing during the war revealed bombs dropped from 8,000ft fell an average of 800ft from the target under ideal conditions. In actual combat the results were even worse.

The USAAC's Engineering Division had initially produced the D-1 bombsight in 1921. Based on a sight designed by inventor Georges Estoppey, the D-1 used a stopwatch to synchronize the speed of the aircraft with the true ground speed and employed a pendulum for stabilization. In 1926 the newly created USAAC adopted a later model of the Estoppey bombsight in the form of the D-4. More robust than the D-1, the D-4 featured an improved internal timing mechanism. When working perfectly in ideal operational conditions, the D-4 achieved good results at altitudes up to 8,000ft, but beyond that bombing errors became excessive.

Desperate to improve results, the USAAC spent a great deal of money (principally with the Sperry Gyroscope Company) on new bombsights before stumbling onto the US Navy's Norden Mk XV in 1931. The latter, developed by Dutch engineer Carl Norden, was a technical marvel, for in clear skies and perfect conditions it could, in theory, cut the average bombing error to something closer to 100ft when combined with an automatic pilot system developed by Sperry for the USAAC. The latter duly placed an order for 45 Mk XVs, at a cost of $4,275 a piece, in April 1932. During training exercises from 1930 to 1938, the USAAC dropped more than 200,000 bombs. Using the Norden bombsight from low altitude (5,000–8,000ft), some crews were able to hit their target within the 100ft range. Above an altitude of 10,000ft, the numbers were more sobering, with most bombs missing by 300–400ft. In actual combat conditions, the Norden did not live up to its lofty expectations and proved to be an expensive failure.

In Britain, meanwhile, development of a new bombsight languished. The RAF entered the war using the obsolete, World War I-era, Mks VII and IX Course Setting Bomb Sights. These were eventually replaced by the Mk XIV Blackett Computing Bomb Sight from 1942, which boasted a mechanical computer and gyro-stabilization. Although slightly less accurate than the Norden Mk XV, the Mk XIV was smaller, easier to use, more immediately responsive to course changes, and generally more suitable for night bombing.

No matter what kind of bombsight was used to hit targets in occupied Europe during World War II, the reality was that when everything went right, only five per cent of the bombs dropped fell within 500 yards of the aiming point and only half struck within 2,000 yards of it.

On 8 August 1934 the USAAC issued Circular 35-25 for a new bomber to replace its fleet of B-10s. The aircraft had to be 'multi-engined' (a term used to denote the use of two engines at the time), with a top speed of 250mph and range of 2,200 miles. Douglas's entry, which became the twin-engined B-18 Bolo, was based on its DC-2 airliner, which had entered service in the USA in May 1934. Martin proposed an improved version of its proven B-10, while Boeing engineers interpreted 'multi-engined' to mean more than two engines and embarked on a far riskier design. Drawing on the streamlining advances made with the commercial Boeing 247 transport (the first of which had flown in February 1933), Boeing's Model 299 bomber prototype was a huge aircraft. Powered by four 750hp Pratt & Whitney R-1690-E Hornet single-row air-cooled radial engines, the new bomber had a wingspan of 104ft and was capable of carrying 4,800lbs of ordnance over a distance of 1,700 miles.

Given the civil registration NX13372, the Model 299 took to the air for the first time on the morning of 28 July 1935. After just 12 days of test flying, the aircraft flew nonstop from Seattle, Washington, to Wright Field, near Dayton, Ohio, the 2,100-mile flight taking a little over nine hours to complete at an average speed of 233mph. The Model 299 was then the world's most advanced bomber, and it was easy to see why. All-metal, streamlined, bristling with defensive armament and capable of carrying a significant bomb load over an unrivalled distance, the new Boeing set the template for all the four-engined bombers that followed in its wake.

Unfortunately for the USAAC, disaster struck when the Model 299 stalled and crashed during take-off as a result of pilot error on 30 October 1935. The resulting crash disqualified Boeing from the contract, with the USAAC subsequently ordering the less advanced B-18. The great potential of the new Boeing bomber was so obvious to the USAAC, however, that it quickly purchased 14 'service test' aircraft – the Model 299's daunting cost precluded the procurement of a larger number of airframes. Designated the Y1B-17 (the 'Y' indicated test model and the '1' denoted the special funding required to cover its acquisition), the new aircraft was powered by four 930hp Wright GR-1820-39 Cyclone engines. Twelve of the YB-17s served with the 2nd BG, and formed the nucleus of US strategic air power. By the time of the Munich Crisis in September 1938, the 2nd BG had flown 1,800,000 miles without serious incident.

The 13th Y1B-17 was delivered to the USAAC's Material Division at Wright Field and used for flight testing, while the 14th example, its engines equipped with General Electric turbo-superchargers, was designated the Y1B-17A. Engine output was boosted to 1,000hp, giving the aircraft an unprecedented service ceiling of 30,000ft. Once service testing had been successfully completed, the 'Y1' prefix was dropped from the aircrafts' designation. An order for 39 follow-on B-17Bs was placed in 1938. The first of these aircraft were delivered to the USAAC in July 1939, equipping the 2nd and 7th BGs. Powered by four 1,200hp nine-cylinder Wright R-1820-51 Cyclone engines, the B-models incorporated a redesigned flat nose panel and larger rudder and flaps. They were followed by 38 B-17Cs, which added a ventral gunner and two waist-mounted weapons firing through teardrop-shaped sliding panels that sat flush with the fuselage, rather than the side gun blisters.

The near-identical B-17D added more armour protection and increased defensive armament, which now consisted of one 0.30-in. and six 0.50-in. machine guns.

During the first 18 months of World War II, the heavy losses experienced by the RAF's bomber squadrons during daylight operations had caused a great deal of consternation within Bomber Command. Holding on to its belief that high altitude and speed offered the best form of protection, the RAF hastily acquired 20 turbo-supercharged B-17Cs – these were christened Fortress Is in British service and issued to No. 90 Sqn. On 8 July 1941, three examples were sent to bomb Wilhelmshaven. Two aircraft found their target, and all returned safely. However, after just 42 sorties (24 of which were abortive), the Fortress I was withdrawn from operational service with Bomber Command, flying its last mission on 8 September. The aircraft had proven a failure with the RAF, which had lost eight Fortress Is – two to enemy fighters and six to other causes.

Just 14 Y1B-17s were built, and 12 of them, including this example having its engines run up, served with the 2nd BG. Powered by four Wright GR-1820-39 Cyclone radials each rated at 930hp for takeoff, the Y1B-17 had a maximum speed of 256mph at 14,000ft and a maximum bombload of 8,000lbs. Parked behind this aircraft is a B-18 Bolo and an A-20 Havoc. (Author's Collection)

B-17F 42-3524

Built at Boeing's Denver plant as a B-17F, 42-3524 was one of the few F-models fitted with a Bendix chin turret as seen on all B-17Gs. The aircraft did, however, retain the F-model's original Sperry dorsal turret, open waist gun positions and the radio operator's gun, although the cheek guns synonymous with the B-17G were absent. Christened *Vonnie Gal*, 42-3524 was the oldest operational Flying Fortress assigned to the 379th BG, based at Kimbolton, Cambridgeshire, by the time fate and flak finally caught up with it during a raid on Leipzig on 20 July 1944. Whilst being flown by 527th BS pilot 2Lt William F. Moore, *Vonnie Gal* was struck by flak over the target seconds after releasing its bombs. With his bomber badly damaged and leaking fuel, Moore pointed its nose in the direction of neutral Switzerland and landed at Payerne airfield shortly thereafter – both the aircraft and its crew were immediately interned. *Vonnie Gal* was eventually patched up and flown back to Burtonwood, in Lancashire, on 25 September 1945, only to be scrapped a few weeks later.

Just as the B-17C was being withdrawn from RAF service, the first B-17Es started to reach the USAAC. The first truly combat-ready Flying Fortress, the E-model was six feet longer than the B-17C and seven tons heavier than the original Model 299. Much of this additional weight took the form of increased defensive armament, with the B-17E boasting eight 0.50-in. machine guns in various locations in the fuselage and a single 0.30-in. weapon in the nose. The guns were mounted in a powered dorsal turret, the tail, in the waist, and in a remotely controlled ventral turret. The B-17E first saw combat with the Eighth Air Force on 17 August 1942, when 12 Flying Fortresses from the 97th BG were escorted by four squadrons of RAF Spitfire IXs in a raid on the Sotteville marshalling yards near Rouen, France. A total of 18 tons of bombs were dropped, with two B-17Es being slightly damaged by flak.

By the autumn of 1942 the vastly improved B-17F had entered service, to be followed by the B-17G in 1943. These two variants, which are described in more detail in the next chapter, would be targeted by the Third Reich's powerful flak and fighter defences through to VE Day.

The USAAF's second heavy bomber in the European Theatre of Operations (ETO) was the B-24 Liberator. In 1938, at the request of the French *Armee de l'Air*, Consolidated had secretly commenced design work on a four-engined bomber. At the same time, the USAAC had begun searching for a new heavy bomber to complement the B-17. With war in Europe on the horizon, US President Franklin D. Roosevelt secured backing from Congress in January 1939 to spend $300,000,000 on the acquisition of new military aircraft. With the B-17 by then already four years old, the USAAC issued a request for a new bomber capable of attaining a speed of 310mph and a ceiling in excess of 30,000ft while carrying a four-ton bomb load up to 3,000 miles.

Consolidated combined their earlier design work on the French bomber with a completely new wing, which would be the key to the aircraft's operational success in myriad roles. Conceived by aeronautical engineer David R. Davis, the new 'Davis' aerofoil promised high lift, less drag and long range at a high cruising speed. Compared to the B-17, the B-24 would have a quicker gestation period. On 30 March 1939, Consolidated was awarded a contract for a single prototype XB-24. One month later the USAAC ordered seven YB-24 service test aircraft, and by 10 August it had committed to a further 38 B-24As.

On 29 December 1939 the XB-24 (39-680) made its first flight from Lindbergh Field in San Diego. Powered by four Pratt & Whitney R-1830-33 Twin Wasp engines, the new bomber, with its Davis wing, had a longer range than the B-17 but its maximum speed (at 273mph) was appreciably slower than expected. Although the French would be the second nation to order the B-24, the country's capitulation to German forces in June 1940 meant the order was never fulfilled. Britain duly took over all outstanding French aircraft contracts, obtaining six YB-24s (designated LB-30As) and 20 B-24As (LB-30Bs) from 1941.

XB-24 prototype 39-556 (later serialled 39-680) flies over southern California during an early test flight from San Diego. The longer-legged Liberator would prove itself in combat in the ETO, where its rugged construction and heavy bombload made the aircraft popular with crews. (Author's Collection)

Like the B-17, the early versions of the B-24 were deficient in armament. In December 1941 the first of nine C-models incorporating a Martin powered turret in the dorsal position and a tail turret, both with two 0.50-in. machine guns, and a single 0.50-in. ventral gun was delivered. Production soon switched to the B-24D, which was the first model to be produced in quantity. Capable of hauling up to 8,000lbs of ordnance, its nominal range with a 5,000lb bomb load was 2,300 miles. Combat experience with the B-24D led to the creation of the H-model, which incorporated the Emerson A-15 nose turret and improved Consolidated A-6B tail turret. The B-24H was quickly followed by the near-definitive Liberator, the B-24J – it was also the most-produced variant, with 6,678 examples completed. Both the H- and J-models were equipped with a retractable Sperry ball turret.

The final versions to see combat were the B-24L/M models, which had been modified to address the excessive weight gain, degraded performance and poor visibility. Lighter tail and ventral ball turrets rectified many of the weight-related issues.

Equipped with increasingly capable versions of the B-17 and B-24 heavy bombers, the Eighth Air Force entered the European air war in the autumn of 1942 with a clear, but unproven vision. Firm in their belief of the self-defending bomber and convinced of their ability to bomb with accuracy, the USAAF dismissed the potential effects of German anti-aircraft defences. However, the advent of radar

On the ground, the Stirling was an imposing aircraft, standing 22ft 9in high. Stirling III EF133 HA-A of No. 218 Sqn participated in Operation *Glimmer* on D-Day, dropping *Window* to simulate an invasion fleet as part of an elaborate deception plan to make the enemy think the actual landings would be made further up the Normandy coast. The aircraft was photographed on a visit to the 34th BG base at Mendlesham, in Suffolk, in the summer of 1944, having just completed 32 operations. It was subsequently transferred to No. 149 Sqn prior to joining No. 1651 HCU in September 1944. EF133 was struck off charge on 25 April 1945. (Author's Collection)

technology and high-performance flak guns meant the air war over Germany would be a long, bloody struggle.

When Boeing's gleaming Model 299 first appeared in July 1935, the British were far behind in the development of a four-engined bomber. For the Air Ministry, the distinction between light, medium and heavy bombers, and what roles they would fill, had yet to be resolved. At the same time Britain's commitment to the League of Nations' series of World Disarmament Conferences in Geneva in 1932–34, which attempted to abolish heavy bombers altogether by imposing weight limits, turned the RAF's bomber procurement into a muddled mess. The resulting new specifications led to the production of such ineffective types as the single-engined Fairey Battle and twin-engined Bristol Blenheim light bombers.

These were followed by the RAF's first twin-engined medium bombers, the Armstrong Whitworth Whitley, Vickers Wellington and Handley Page Hampden. All three designs appeared in 1936, making their first flights between March and June. While modern in construction, none of the medium bombers could deliver adequate bomb loads to distant targets such as Berlin. The Third Reich's rapid rearmament programme and the threat it posed to peace in Europe caused the Air Ministry to issue a new set of specifications for a second generation of monoplane medium and heavy bombers capable of conducting strategic bombing operations over Germany.

In the same month (July 1936) RAF Bomber Command was formed, the Air Ministry issued Specification B.12/36 for a new, heavy, four-engined bomber. Performance requirements included carriage of a maximum bombload of 14,000lb over a range of 2,000 miles, or 8,000lb up to 3,000 miles. It was a revolutionary step forward, but as was typical of the bureaucratic muddling that blighted the RAF at this time, staff officers stated that they wanted a single new day/night bomber that was capable of also performing secondary roles such as reconnaissance, troop transportation and torpedo-bombing.

At the same time, the Air Ministry, eager to develop a new twin-engined medium bomber with enhanced capabilities, issued specification P.13/36 in August 1936. Through luck and serendipity, this would lead directly to the development of Britain's best heavy bombers of World War II, the Handley Page Halifax and Avro Lancaster.

Seven contenders put forth proposals for Specification B.12/36, with Vickers and Supermarine being the favourites. In the end, Short and Supermarine were awarded contracts for two prototypes. During the Battle of Britain, Supermarine's two incomplete Type 318 airframes and associated construction plans were lost when the company's Woolston works was bombed on 26 September 1940. This left Short's S.29 with a clear field. The first prototype of what would become the Stirling bomber had in fact commenced flight trials as early as mid-May 1939.

Powered by four 1,375hp Bristol Hercules II radial engines, each equipped with a single-speed supercharger, the ungainly looking Stirling towered above the ground standing 22ft 9in high. In terms of performance, the Stirling was a leap forward for the RAF, but it suffered from a low maximum ceiling of just 17,000ft. At that height German 88mm and 105mm flak guns could engage the bomber sooner and for a longer period of time, resulting in heavier than expected losses. The Stirling I flew its first combat mission on 10/11 February 1941, when three aircraft from No. 7 Sqn attacked oil storage tanks at Rotterdam. By mid-1943 the Stirling equipped 12 squadrons in Bomber Command. After almost three years on operations, more than 700 Stirlings (of the 2,371 examples built) had been lost to flak and fighters.

While authorising the development of the Stirling, the Air Ministry was also interested in a bomber powered by a pair of Rolls-Royce Vulture engines. As noted earlier in this chapter, in August 1936 Specification P.13/36 was issued, calling for a new medium bomber. Only three companies vied for the new contract, Handley Page, Avro and Vickers. The latter dropped out in favour of developing the Warwick, an

Two Halifax B IIs from No. 35 Sqn undertake a training mission from their airfield at Linton-on-Ouse, in North Yorkshire, during the early summer of 1942. Both aircraft are fully equipped with three Bolton Paul powered turrets, including the rather large and drag-inducing Type C mid-upper turret. In the foreground is Halifax W7676/TL-P, which failed to return from a raid on Nuremburg on the night of 28/29 August 1942. (Author's Collection)

Stirling I BK611

Stirling I BK611/LS-U was delivered to No. 15 Sqn at RAF Mildenhall, Suffolk, on 24 December 1942 and named *Te Kooti* after the famous Maori chief, with nose art painted beneath the pilot's window. An unusual mission tally was recorded on the rear fuselage between the crew door and the serial. The aircraft's pilot, Australian Sgt J. O. Wilson, and bomb aimer Sgt P. Arnott were killed when *Te Kooti* was shot down by flak returning from an operation to Düsseldorf on 25/26 May 1943, the bomber crashing at Grubbenvorst, in Holland. Five of the crew managed to briefly evade before being captured by German troops. A total of 27 aircraft (eight of which were Stirlings) were lost on this raid from a force of 759 bombers. Cloud cover over the target rendered the attack a failure, with bombs being scattered over a wide area.

improved version of the Wellington. In what proved to be a fortunate twist of fate, an inadequate supply of Vulture engines allied with its poor reliability record led directly to the development of the Handley Page Halifax and Avro Lancaster, Britain's best heavy bombers. If Specification P.13/36 had called for aircraft to be fitted with Rolls-Royce Merlins or Bristol Hercules engines instead of the Vulture, these heavy bombers may never have been built.

On 30 April 1937, two prototypes (Avro Type 679 and Handley Page HP.56), each to be powered by the Vulture engine, were ordered. When it became clear Rolls-Royce was going to struggle to build sufficient Vulture engines to fulfil Air Ministry orders, Handley Page decided its new bomber would have to be redesigned for fitment with four Merlin engines instead. Avro also wanted to switch to the proven Merlin, but the Air Ministry was afraid of delaying delivery of its urgently needed medium bomber (christened the Manchester) still further and ordered the company to stick with the Vulture.

Designated HP.57 and later given the name Halifax, the new Handley Page heavy bomber was fitted with four 1,145hp Merlin X engines. The first hand-built and unarmed prototype made its maiden flight on 25 October 1939, with the second, armed (Bolton Paul Type C turret with two 0.303-in. machine guns in the nose and a four-gun Bolton Paul Type E turret in the tail), prototype taking to the air on 17 August 1940. Two months later, the first production variant appeared, designated the Halifax B I Series I. Entering service in November 1940, the Halifax was the most modern bomber operated by the RAF to date, and it also proved to be one of its most versatile. In terms of performance, the early Halifax I was only marginally better than the Stirling I, but it had more room for improvement than the Short bomber. Six major variants would follow during a production run that saw 6,176 aircraft built over a six-year period, with the Hercules-powered Halifax B III obtaining the best performance figures of them all.

Like the Halifax, the Avro Lancaster owed its existence to the unreliable Rolls-Royce 24-cylinder Vulture engine, which promised 1,750hp but in reality could only deliver around 1,450hp. Starting in 1937, it would take Avro two years to construct its Type 679 prototype, with its first flight taking place on 25 July 1939. Flight testing quickly confirmed the fears surrounding the Vulture engine, with reduced power, overheating and mechanical failures being commonplace. In spite of these problems, preparations for quantity production were made before the prototypes had even flown due to the imminent prospect of war with Germany.

The first Manchester IAs were delivered to the RAF in early August 1940. Carrying a crew of seven, the RAF's new medium bomber had a maximum bombload of 10,350lbs and a range of 1,200 miles. Prior to the prototype making its first flight, Avro knew that the Manchester's chances of success as an operational bomber would be dashed by its poor Vulture engines. Keen to ensure that Avro remained at the forefront of the 'bomber business', the company's chief designer, Roy Chadwick, ordered some of his staff to work on a four-engined variant of the Manchester I (designated the Type 683 or Manchester III) fitted with less powerful (1,145hp) but more reliable Rolls-Royce Merlin Xs.

The fall of France in June 1940 put Britain's fate in sharp focus. Rather than tolerate the unreliable Manchester, the Ministry of Aircraft Production (MAP) reduced the number to be built to just 200 aircraft and directed Avro to shift production to the Halifax. Reluctant to build a rival design under licence, Avro convinced MAP that its four-engined Type 683 could be ready within six months. Taking a newly-built Manchester I airframe, Avro increased the wingspan by ten feet in order to make room for the four Merlins. Avro was able to complete the new prototype by early January 1941, just prior to the Manchester I flying its first operational mission.

Thanks to the maturity of its Merlin X powerplants, the prototype Lancaster proved extremely reliable. It had double the range of the Manchester and a bombload that was 35 per cent greater. Testing through the spring of 1941 revealed that the new bomber was also superior to both the Stirling and Halifax. Production, however, was slow, with the first Lancaster I being delivered to No. 44 Sqn in December 1941. This unit gave the aircraft its operational debut three months later.

The Lancaster was the bomber the RAF had been looking for, the aircraft soon proving itself to be a superb 'bomb truck'. Avro had designed the bomber around its huge 33ft-long bomb-bay, which was 11ft longer than the bomb-bay in the Halifax. Furthermore, the Lancaster was able to carry 14 1,000lb bombs or larger weapons like the 4,000lb 'cookie'. By comparison, the Stirling was unable to carry a bomb larger than 2,000lbs within its bomb-bay.

Like the Stirling and Halifax, the Lancaster was designed as a general-purpose day bomber, with an emphasis on powered turrets as a defence against fighter attack.

By the time the aircraft began operations in the spring of 1942, Bomber Command was fully committed to nocturnal attacks. All three of its heavy bombers were not optimized for the nocturnal role, however. And while the effective ceiling of the Lancaster was slightly higher than that of the Halifax, no significant analysis was done regarding the continued development of Germany's flak defences, and the dangers they posed. For the British 'heavies', the narrow height band width in which they operated proved lethal. Due to its low maximum ceiling, the Stirling suffered the most losses proportionally due to flak, followed by the Halifax and Lancaster.

GERMAN DEFENCES

Just as the USAAC and RAF were forging ahead with their strategic bombing strategies and technological advancements during the 1930s, the German armed forces were not far behind. During the same period, and despite the Treaty of Versailles, senior officers within the *Reichswehr* turned their attention to the role of the strategic bomber in a future war. While Germany's development of a four-engined strategic bomber (in the form of the Dornier Do 19) ended in 1936, its focus on the issues of ground-based defences against any future attacks by such an aircraft had begun long before that.

The most numerous heavy anti-aircraft gun in the *Flakwaffe* was the famous 88mm weapon, which served as the basis for four principal variants. It was also the most mobile. Here, a gun crew and battery prepare to fire their camouflaged FlaK 37 weapon from a standard reinforced 88mm *Flak Gefechtsstand* (G-Stand) 1943-pattern gun pit. (Author's Collection)

In 1929, professional military literature in Germany examined the subject of air defence with a renewed and pointed interest. Between October 1929 and March 1930, the leading weekly military journal *Militar-Wochenblatt* published a number of articles that focused on air defence and the development of anti-aircraft guns. One specific article entitled 'Air Defence of German Industry' played on German fears of air attack in the next war. It described how massive 'air fleets' could have the potential to 'bomb Germany to its knees', and it offered a number of prescient defensive measures that could be taken to prevent this. First and foremost was the development of effective heavy anti-aircraft guns. Other methods that could be used included the employment of smoke generators to obscure key industrial sites, searchlights to blind pilots of attacking bombers, establishment of an effective early warning system, the construction of bomb shelters and training factory workers in emergency first aid and firefighting.

The Luftwaffe would subsequently implement each of these measures during World War II.

In February 1930 the *Reichswehr* established the *Flakartillerie* under the command of Oberstleutnant Günther Rüdel, who was responsible for the secret reorganization and rearmament of the flak forces. One of his first priorities was the acquisition of an 88mm heavy gun to replace the increasingly ineffective FlaK L/60 75mm anti-aircraft weapon then in service. Rüdel was keenly aware of the fact that new aircraft required less time to develop and build than flak guns, and their associated equipment. In the development of Germany's air defence system, Rüdel identified three 'special factors' crucial to its future success. The first priority was a weapon capable of engaging aircraft between 33,000–39,000ft travelling at 375mph. Secondly, gunners had to be able to effectively engage aircraft flying on instruments in the dark or above solid cloud cover. Thirdly, he identified the increased use of armour plating within aircraft, which would result in future bombers being able to absorb more flak damage.

FlaK 18

25ft 0in.

7ft 11in.

7ft 6in.

...commenced production of its 88mm
...8 in January 1933, the weapon being derived
...s 8.8cm FlaK 16 gun of World War I. The
...ous semi-automatic loading system resulted
...xcellent rate of fire of 15–20 rounds per
.... The 88mm FlaK series of guns (18, 36 and
...re the mainstay of the *Flakwaffe*, and by
...1944 close to 11,000 were in service across
...ny and occupied Europe.

Rüdel's foresight was in some ways remarkable. The RAF's most elusive bomber, the de Havilland Mosquito, attained a maximum speed of 380mph with a service ceiling of 34,500ft. In contrast, the mainstays of the Allied heavy bomber force – the Lancaster, B-17 and B-24 – were limited to a maximum speed of approximately 290mph. With full bomb loads, the Lancaster had a ceiling of just 24,500ft, the B-17 30,000ft (it rarely flew above this height) and the B-24 24,000ft.

The key problem facing anti-aircraft gun defences between the wars was the need for accurate targeting of enemy bombers. Advances in aviation technology had resulted in the development of aircraft capable of greater speeds and higher ceilings, thus making unaided optical targeting obsolete. A computing device capable of rapidly providing an accurate fire solution was therefore required. In 1925, the German firm Zeiss received a contract for a new optical range finder. A year later, Zeiss also commenced work

As formidable as they were, only 33 128mm Falkzwilling 40/2s had been deployed by 1945. Principally sited atop specially-built flak towers in Berlin, Vienna and Hamburg, these guns were manned by the *Flakwaffe*'s best troops. This example is mounted on the *Gefechtsturm IV* tower in the Heiligengeistfeld district of Hamburg. (NARA)

on a new fire director system. The first operational fire director (*Kommandogerät* P 27) entered service in 1930, and by the outbreak of World War II the improved *Kommandogerät* P 40 fire director had been issued to the *Flakartillerie*. A combination optical range finder and ballistic computer, the P 40 required five crew to man it – two to track azimuth and elevation, a third for slant range, a fourth for horizontal angle of approach and a fifth to operate the various switches. During daylight and good weather, optical targeting procedures using a fire director like the P 40 remained the most effective method of tracking high-altitude targets.

As previously noted, the increased performance of future bomber designs also meant that the *Flakartillerie* urgently needed to acquire a heavy weapon with sufficient muzzle velocity to hit aircraft at greater ceilings than the FlaK L/60 75mm anti-aircraft gun then in service. In anticipation of this, the Germans secretly developed their own 88mm gun. Derived from their World War I 8.8cm FlaK 16 gun, the new 88mm Flak 18, again designed and built by Krupp, proved a huge success. This was followed by the improved FlaK 36, 37 and 41 models.

In August 1937 Rüdel released a report entitled 'Development Programme for the Flak Artillery, 1937'. Designed to prepare the air defences for the coming conflict, the document placed a major emphasis on increasing the muzzle velocity of all German flak guns. This led directly to the development of the new 105mm and mammoth 128mm weapons. Development of the FlaK 38 and 39 105mm guns commenced in 1933, with the first examples reaching the *Flakartillerie* in the spring of 1938. The weapons resembled scaled-up versions of the 88mm FlaK 18, being both heavier and bulkier. Their muzzle velocity of 2,891ft per second and effective ceiling of 31,005ft was slightly greater than the FlaK 18's muzzle velocity of 2,690ft per second and effective ceiling of 26,248ft. Overall, although the performance of the FlaK 38 and

39 was not as good as had been hoped for, they were still formidable weapons that were more than capable of taking on high-flying B-17s.

Despite the somewhat improved performance of the 105mm guns, the Luftwaffe initiated the development of an even larger weapon in the form of the 128mm FlaK 40 for the *Flakartillerie* in 1936. Weighing in at more than 26 tons, the new Rheinmetall-Borsig 128mm gun consumed a vast amount of raw materials in its construction. However, the FlaK 40's performance was remarkable, the gun boasting a muzzle velocity of 2,887ft per second and an effective ceiling of more than 35,000ft. Because of its size and weight, the new 128mm weapon was restricted to firing from fixed sites or rail cars. Following the commencement of full-scale production in 1942, the FlaK 40 was joined by the 128mm Flakzwilling 40/2. Consisting of two guns mounted side-by-side on the same mounting, the twin gun configuration offered exceptional firepower. The Flakzwilling 40/2s were principally sited in flak towers.

Aside from the key German anti-aircraft guns, Axis forces in Europe also employed the Italian Cannone da 90/53 90mm weapon. Designed and built by Ansaldo, it was based on a weapon originally created for warships of the Regia Marina. In service from 1939, the Cannone da 90/53 was closely comparable to the best British and German guns of the period. Indeed, the weapon was so highly valued by the *Flakartillerie* that many captured examples were sent back to Germany after the Italian surrender in September 1943 and re-designated as 9cm FlaK 41(i)s or Flak 309/1(i)s.

It was not just the heavy flak guns that would engage Allied heavy bombers. Light and medium weapons would also play an effective role, especially against low-lying heavy bombers undertaking precision missions such as the Dams Raid on 16–17 May 1943 and the Ploesti campaign. The Luftwaffe's principal light and medium flak guns consisted of the 20mm FlaK 30/38/39 and 37mm FlaK 18/36/37.

By the summer of 1937, Rüdel was keen to further expand the technological development of both flak guns and their aiming and tracking systems. His appreciation of the need for effective night defences was prescient, and he stated at the time that 'the combat of night bomber attacks is the most important task of the air defence'. The Luftwaffe's principal device for detecting bombers and aiming searchlights at night was the *Ringtrichter Richtungshorer* (RRH) sound detector. Limited in its efficiency, the RRH's reliability and accuracy could be adversely affected by weather conditions, including humidity, aircraft flying at higher altitudes and ambient noise levels associated with combat.

Priority was given to the development of both infrared and radar tracking systems. At the beginning of the war the German Kriegsmarine had eight *Freya* radar stations operating along the northern coast of Germany. Although *Freya* was capable of

Although prototypes of the 88mm FlaK 41 had commenced test-firing in early 1941, the weapon did not enter operational service until March 1943. A well-trained 12-men crew could, under ideal conditions, achieve a rate of fire of 20 rounds per minute with the FlaK 41. Boasting a muzzle velocity of 3,280 feet per second, the gun could engage all RAF and USAAF heavy bombers in the ETO, as well as high-flying Allied escort fighters. (National Museum of the USAF)

identifying approaching aircraft at a distance of up to 120 miles, it was unable to provide altitude or precise position values to allow contacts to be accurately engaged by flak batteries. With the commencement of nocturnal raids by Bomber Command on German industrial targets in the late summer of 1940, the *Flakartillerie* desperately needed an effective way to allow its gunners to engage bombers at night. This expedited the creation of two radar systems in the form of the Lorenz FuMG 40L and Telefunken's *Würzburg*.

The Lorenz system had a range of 15–25 miles and an accuracy under ideal conditions of plus or minus 12–15 yards. The *Würzburg* radar had almost double the range, but was less accurate. With the latter system being more readily available, Telefunken won the contract. The first FuMG 39T(C) *Würzburg* gun-laying radars finally entered service in the summer of 1941. A lack of foresight in respect to the importance of this technology would cost the Luftwaffe dearly, as a continual shortage of gun-laying radar meant that RRH sound detectors never fully disappeared – in 1944 there were still 5,560 of them in service.

Between 1933 and 1938 Luftwaffe flak forces experienced an unprecedented expansion, resulting in more than 70,000 men serving in the *Flakartillerie* and searchlight and barrage balloon batteries by 1939. It would be their job to protect the 2,359 important armaments-related targets (aircraft and tank assembly plants, munitions factories and military installations) within the Third Reich that the Luftwaffe had identified could be attacked by enemy bombers upon the outbreak of war. With so many sites to protect, the Luftwaffe found itself with a major disparity between planned and projected flak gun strength. Pre-war production had so far failed to meet the *Flakartillerie*'s growing demand, prompting Hitler himself to order an increase in production of the 88mm gun and all other ancillary equipment in July 1939.

By the time German troops rolled into Poland on the morning of 1 September 1939, the Luftwaffe's flak strength had risen to 657 heavy flak batteries (2,628 88mm and 105mm guns), 560 light flak batteries (6,700 20mm and 37mm flak guns) and 188 searchlight batteries (2,052 60cm searchlights). Also included in these numbers were three Wehrmacht-controlled railway flak gun battalions and seven Kriegsmarine naval flak battalions.

On the eve of war, Germany had the finest and most formidable air defences in the world. Günther Rüdel, who by now had attained the rank of *General der Flakartillerie*, was so optimistic that he proclaimed 'the flak artillery will be the decisive factor in the war of the future'.

This close up view of an abandoned 88mm FlaK 36 gun south of Caen clearly shows the 'follow the pointer' dials to the left of the gun shield. Up-to-the-minute targeting information from the central command post would be relayed to the gunners, who then set the dials prior to firing. Two crewmen controlled the elevation and azimuth of the gun when tracking a target. Fire control information was fed electrically to the gun, which resulted in one of the coloured pointers moving to a determined setting. Two crewmen then simply positioned the gun at the correct angle of elevation and azimuth, matching the second set of pointers with those sent by the fire director, before firing. (Author's Collection)

TECHNICAL SPECIFICATIONS

USAAF HEAVY BOMBERS

FORTRESS I (B-17C)

The B-17C (albeit in Fortress I guise, serving with the RAF) was the first American four-engined heavy bomber to attack German targets during World War II. In the spring of 1941 the RAF received 20 B-17Cs, which were supplied to No. 90 Sqn. Equipped with turbo-supercharged 1,000hp Wright R-1820-65 Cyclone engines, Bomber Command was eager to use the Fortress I at high altitude, convinced it would make the aircraft immune from interception by enemy fighters.

The bomber had an impressive top speed of 300mph at 29,000ft and a cruising speed of 230mph. With a crew of seven, the Fortress I was armed with six Browning M2 0.50-in. machine guns and one Browning AN-M2 0.30-in. weapon. Capable of carrying just four 1,100lb bombs, the aircraft had a combat radius of 450 miles.

After just 26 raids, the surviving Fortress Is were withdrawn in September 1941. By then a total of eight aircraft had been were lost to all causes, with two downed by fighters and none by flak. In total, 38 B-17Cs were built.

Boeing B-17 F („Fortress II")

Kampfflugzeug

Die Panzer sind außer dem mit 20mm angegebenen, 6,4mm.

je 1tem MG. Cal. 'Kal. 12,7mm

je 1tem MG. Cal. 'Kal. 12,7mm

1tem MG. Cal. 'Kal. 16mm

1tem Doppel-MG. Cal. 'Kal. 12,7mm 1tem MG. Cal. 'Kal. 12,7mm 20mm Panzerplx ~50mm

1tem Doppel-MG. Cal. 'Kal. 12,7mm

Die Bewaffnung besteht aus 11×12,7 mm-MG. und 1×7,6 mm-MG. Mit Ausnahme der beiden kraftgesteuerten Drehtürme auf Rumpfoberseite und Rumpfunterseite werden alle Waffen durch Hand betätigt

Taken from a Luftwaffe aircraft identification manual, this three-view drawing of a B-17F clearly shows the location of armour plating, self-sealing fuel tanks (in red) and defensive armament. American heavy bombers were well armed and armoured, which in turn meant that they were able to remain airworthy despite often sustaining extensive damage from flak and fighters. (Author's Collection)

B-17E

The RAF always considered the B-17C to be 'overgunned and under-bombed', and in many respects this was true. Effectively conceived as a medium bomber, its payload was just 4,400lbs. Known simply as the 'Seventeen' to American crewmen, the new B-17E had been significantly redesigned by Boeing – the company claimed that 30 per cent of its structure differed from the D-model, which was essentially the version of the B-17C flown by the USAAC. Most evident was the E-model's enlarged tailplane and distinctive, sweeping fillet that began halfway along the fuselage.

The first B-17Es assigned to the USAAF arrived in England in July 1942, these aircraft being armed with eight 0.50-in. machines guns and a single 0.30-in. calibre weapon in the nose. More armour was added, but none of it was placed to protect the engines or crew from the effects of flak. With a fuselage some 73ft 10in. in length and wings spanning of 103ft 9in., the B-17E was powered by four Wright-Cyclone R-1820-65 engines capable of 1,200hp apiece. They gave the aircraft a maximum speed of 317mph at 25,000ft. The E-model had a fuel capacity of 2,780 gallons, giving it a range of 2,000 miles.

A total of 812 B-17Es were ordered, but only 512 were completed.

B-17F

Production of the B-17F began in May 1942. Outwardly, it differed little from the E-model, with the bomber's most distinguishing features being the more pointed, single-piece Plexiglas nose glazing and an increased number of defensive guns (12 0.50-in. machine guns). However, internally, Boeing had made more than 400 changes that improved its combat effectiveness by increasing the aircraft's range and load-carrying capacity. Uprated Wright R-1820-97 Cyclone engines were fitted, which could generate 1,380hp if War-Emergency boost was selected – they drove new paddle-bladed propellers. Additional fuel tanks increased range to 1,500 miles with a 4,000–5,000lb bombload.

A total of 3,405 B-17Es were built in three plants during a production run that lasted just 15 months.

B-17G

Along with the F-model, the B-17G was the primary variant of Boeing's venerable Flying Fortress family to see combat with the Eighth Air Force in the ETO – it was also widely used by the Fifteenth Air Force in the daylight bombing campaign against the Third Reich, flying from bases in Italy. The final production variant of the Flying Fortress, it included all of the various design changes incorporated into the F-model, principally in response to the increased threat posed by German fighters making head-on attacks. The key addition was the new remotely-operated Bendix 'chin' turret armed with two 0.50-in. machine guns. The Sperry top turret was also replaced by a Bendix unit, while a new Cheyenne turret was installed in the tail – both positions were again fitted with two M2 machine guns apiece. Due to the added weight associated with four powered turrets and 13 machine guns, the B-17G's maximum speed dropped to 287mph at 25,000ft.

A total of 8,680 G-models were built between August 1943 and July 1945.

B-24D

Built in greater quantity than any other American combat aircraft, the Liberator has often been overshadowed by the more famous B-17. Dimensionally similar to the Flying Fortress, the Liberator was easily recognizable thanks to its long, thin Davis wing, twin rudders, tricycle landing gear and box-like fuselage.

Powered by four Pratt & Whitney R-1830-43 engines, each rated at 1,200hp, the D-model of the Liberator was only the second American heavy bomber to see combat over Europe. While more demanding to fly than the B-17E/F, the B-24D had a superior range and bigger bombload. Maximum speed was 303mph at 25,000ft. With a more spacious bomb-bay, the B-24D could carry up to 8,800lbs of ordnance. This was reduced to 5,000lbs when covering distances of up to 2,300 miles. Like the B-17E, the B-24D was equipped with self-sealing fuel tanks and armour plating for each crew station. Although the armament installed in the D-model varied during the aircraft's production run, typically, most examples were fitted with ten 0.50-in. M2 machine guns. Only four of the latter were turret-mounted, split evenly between the Martin A-3 dorsal and Consolidated A-6 tail turrets.

B-24Ds began to reach the USAAC in January 1942, and by the time production of this variant ended, 2,696 had been built. Like later models of the Flying Fortress, the Liberator was equipped with self-sealing fuel tanks and armour plating for each crew station.

B-24G-1

Just 405 G-1s were built, this variant effectively being a B-24D with an A-6 turret in the nose to offer the aircraft better protection from head-on attacks by German fighters. B-24G-1s served primarily with Fifteenth Air Force units in Italy.

B-24H

The H-model was the first major production model equipped with the Emerson A-15 turret in place of the B-24D's 24-panel 'greenhouse' nose glazing. More than 50 other airframe changes were also made, with the more obvious ones being a

B-24M 44-50443 of the Fifteenth Air Force's 727th BS/451st BG releases its bombs over the railway marshalling yards at Mühldorf, in Bavaria, on 19 March 1945. The M-model Liberator was essentially a lightweight B-24J, with 2,593 examples being built in 1944–45. (USAF)

redesigned bombardier's compartment (as a direct result of the turret installation), improved visibility from the dorsal and tail turrets and Plexiglas panelled, laterally offset, waist gun positions. The D-model's R-1830-43 engines were retained, however. A total of 3,100 B-24Hs were built.

B-24J

Built in greater numbers (6,678) than any other Liberator variant, the J-model went into series production from August 1943. A shortage of Emerson turrets meant that most B-24Js were fitted with modified A-6 turrets instead. Although very similar to the H-model, the B-24J was in many ways inferior to its predecessor. Drag from the front turret and an overall increase in weight to 65,000lbs made it 5,000lbs heavier than the D-model. This in turn meant that the aircraft was slower (even with its upgraded Pratt & Whitney R-1830-65 engines) and had to fly at a lower altitude than previous models.

B-24L/M

Concerned by the drop in performance of the heavily armed B-24H/J, the USAAF asked Consolidated to build a lighter version of the Liberator. The company responded with the B-24L, which was 1,000lbs lighter than the preceding model through the removal of the Sperry ventral ball turret and replacement of the hydraulically powered Consolidated A-6B rear turret with the manually powered M-6A. The B-24M was similar to the L-model, with additional weight savings and a redesigned flightdeck canopy to improve the pilot's vision for formation flying. The A-6B turret, in lightweight form, was reintroduced, as was the Sperry ball turret. Finally, the waist gunner positions were also left open.

A total of 1,667 B-24Ls and 2,593 B-24Ms were completed in 1944–45.

RAF HEAVY BOMBERS

STIRLING I
Production of Britain's first heavy bomber was extremely slow, with just 15 delivered by the end of 1940 and 21 in the first quarter of 1941. While capable of carrying an impressive load of seven 2,000lb or eight 500lb bombs, the Stirling's overall performance was mediocre. Powered by four Bristol Hercules XI radial engines rated at 1,590hp, the Mk I had a top speed of just 260mph at 10,500ft and a range of barely 740 miles with a full bomb load of 14,000lbs. Because of its short wing span (99ft 1in) and single-stage supercharged engines, the Stirling's maximum ceiling was limited to 17,000ft. A fully loaded Mk I, however, was hard pressed to reach 12,000ft, making it highly vulnerable to light, medium and heavy flak.

STIRLING III
To address the Stirling's poor performance at altitude the Mk III was introduced in 1943, powered by 1,635hp Bristol Hercules Mk VI or XVI engines. Although the bomber's top speed increased to 270mph, the Stirling III still struggled to match the Lancaster and Halifax in respect of its performance at high altitude. It was rapidly replaced in Bomber Command as a result.

At the Stirling's peak in 1943, just 13 bomber squadrons were equipped with the aircraft. A total of 2,383 Stirlings were built between 1939–45, of which 756 were Mk Is and 875 were Mk IIIs.

HALIFAX B I
Although often viewed as the 'poor cousin' of the Lancaster because of its inferior bombload and service ceiling, the Halifax's performance was not that far short of the Avro bomber. It was also more versatile and had a better crew survival rate. Entering service in 1940, the Halifax was the most modern bomber the RAF had ever seen. The B I was powered by four 1,280hp Merlin X engines that gave the aircraft a top speed of 265mph at 17,500ft. Maximum bombload was 14,500lbs, and the Mk I could reach an altitude of 22,000ft. Armament consisted of six 0.303-in. machine guns, with two in a Boulton Paul Type C nose turret, four in a Boulton Paul Type K tail turret and two in waist positions. Just 84 B Is were built.

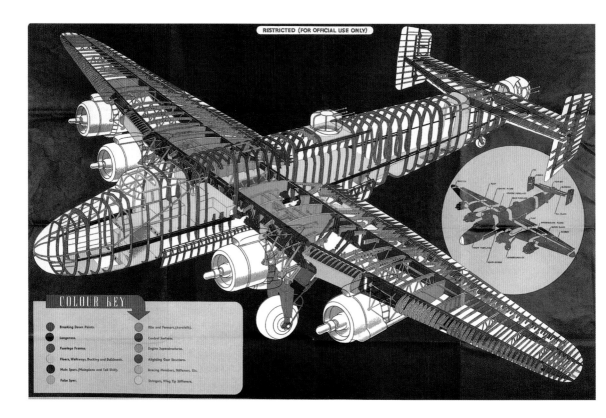

COLOUR KEY

Breaking Down Points.
Longerons.
Fuselage Frames.
Floors, Walkways, Ducking and Bulkheads.
Main Spars.(Mainplane and Tail Unit).
False Spar.

Ribs and Formers.(Aerofoils).
Control Surfaces.
Engine Superstructures.
Alighting Gear Structure.
Bracing Members, Stiffeners, Etc.
Stringers, Wing Tip Stiffeners.

This cutaway drawing shows the main structure of the Halifax B III. Thanks to its larger fuselage and well-placed escape hatches (particularly the one in the underside of the nose), the Halifax had a better crew survival rate compared to the more famous Lancaster. Twenty-nine per cent of Halifax aircrew shot down survived, while for the Lancaster, the figure was just 11 per cent. (Author's Collection

HALIFAX B II/V

The B I's defensive armament was soon shown to be woefully inadequate, so Handley Page added a Bolton Paul Type C (or a Type A) twin gun dorsal turret and the waist guns were deleted. Fuel capacity was also increased by 15 per cent and the new variant was fitted with Merlin XXs rated at 1,390hp. The Merlin-engined Halifax was never a graceful aircraft, its bulbous nose turrets, heavily framed bomb aimer's position and large dorsal turret creating excessive drag that degraded performance. When fully loaded, the aircraft developed a tendency to spin uncontrollably. Heavy losses in combat and dangerous spins led to radical design changes.

In an effort to eradicate some of the weight and drag problems associated with the standard B II handling problems, Handley Page created the B II Series I (Special) through the deletion of the nose and dorsal turrets. Performance increased by some ten per cent, but there was still room for improvement. This took the form of the B II Series IA, which was stripped of all but essential equipment. It featured a streamlined Perspex nose fairing, a new Bolton-Paul low-drag four-gun dorsal turret and a semi-retractable tailwheel. The fuselage was increased in length by 1ft 6in, 1,620hp Merlin 24 engines installed and the original triangular tailfins replaced by larger rectangular units, which were found to dampen yaw and thus improve bombing accuracy. The B V, which entered service from May 1943, was similarly configured to the B II Series IA, although it was fitted with four Merlin XXs rated at 1,480hp.

From September 1943, units equipped with B IIs experienced a sharp increase in combat attrition because they were unable to attain altitudes exceeding 20,000ft. This in turn made the B IIs easier prey for nightfighters and both medium and heavy flak. Bomber Command was forced to restrict the aircraft to attacks on less hazardous targets.

A total of 1,977 B IIs and 904 B Vs were completed by five manufacturers.

HALIFAX B III/VI

The introduction of the Hercules-powered B III transformed the Halifax's performance. Fitted with four 1,615hp Bristol Hercules VI radial engines driving de Havilland Hydromatic propellers, the aircraft's maximum speed (at normal loaded weight) was increased to 282mph at 13,500ft and its service ceiling at maximum load to 22,000ft. Entering service in October 1943, the B III – which retained the Perspex nose and modified tail of the B II Series IA, but with the addition of rounded wingtips that increased bombing altitude by 2,000ft – allowed Halifax squadrons to hit the enemy's most heavily defended targets once more.

Closely related to the B III, the B VI of early 1945 was the final bomber variant, being powered by four 1,630hp Bristol Hercules 100 engines and boasting increased fuel capacity. A total of 2,091 B IIIs and 473 B VIs were built for the RAF in 1943–45.

The design of the Lancaster revolved around its huge 33ft-long bomb-bay, which could carry 14 1,000lb bombs or larger weapons like the 4,000lb 'cookie'. In contrast, the Halifax had only a 22ft-long bomb-bay, and the Stirling could not carry any weapon larger than a 2,000lb bomb. The Lancaster's ability to carry large bombloads quickly made it the preferred aircraft of Bomber Command. (Imperial War Museum, CH 18554)

LANCASTER B I

The famed Lancaster was rightly considered to be the best British heavy bomber of the war. In terms of bombload and performance it was far superior to the Stirling I/III and the Halifax II/Vs.

Entering service in December 1941, the Lancaster B I was powered by four 1,460hp Rolls-Royce Merlin XX engines, each fitted with a single-stage supercharger. When carrying a typical bombload of 12,000lbs of ordnance, the B I had a maximum speed of 275mph and a service ceiling of 24,500ft. Typical cruising speed was 230mph, with an operational range of between 1,730 and 2,530 miles, depending on bombload. What set the Lancaster apart from other British heavy bombers was its voluminous bomb-bay. At 33ft long, it could carry 14 1,000lb bombs, or larger weapons like the 4,000lb and 8,000lb 'Cookie' bombs. Finally, with modifications to its bomb-bay, the aircraft (in B I Special form) could accommodate a single 22,000lb Grand Slam bomb. This versatility of load, coupled with a good turn of speed, unmatched service ceiling and adequate defensive armament (eight 0.303-in. machine guns split between three Frazer Nash hydraulically operated nose, dorsal and tail turrets), quickly made the Lancaster the preferred aircraft of Bomber Command.

In total, 3,425 B Is were built between November 1941 and March 1946.

LANCASTER B II

Fearing a shortage of Merlin engines, MAP also sourced an alternate powerplant for the Lancaster B I in the form of 1,735hp Bristol Hercules VI or XVI radial engines. Production of the aircraft, designated the B III, commenced in September 1942, the bomber being essentially similar to the B I bar its radial engines and slightly enlarged bomb-bay. The Merlin shortage proved to be illusory, resulting in just 301 B IIIs being

Canadian-built Lancaster X KB712/VL-R *S for Smitty* of No. 419 Sqn RCAF undergoes engine power checks at RAF Middleton St George, in County Durham, in the spring of 1944. During an operation in July of that year, KB712 was caught in the glare of six or seven searchlights over the Ruhr. Despite receiving flak damage to the bomb-bay doors, fuselage and engine nacelles, the bomber was nursed home by Plt Off George Hartford. KB712 was eventually shot down, with the loss of its entire crew, on the 28 October 1944 raid on Cologne. (Author's Collection)

built by the time production ended in March 1944. These aircraft were split between four Royal Canadian Air Force (RCAF) and two RAF squadrons.

LANCASTER B III

Identical to the B I, the B III was powered by Packard-built 1,460hp Merlin 28 and 38 engines rather than Rolls-Royce Merlin XXs. A total of 3,039 were completed between November 1942 and June 1945.

LANCASTER B X

Constructed in Malton, Ontario, by Victory Aircraft Limited, the Canadian-built B X was based on the B III. Equipped with 1,460hp Packard Merlin 244 engines, the B X also had US-made instrumentation and electrics. On later batches of the aircraft, the mid-upper Nash & Thompson FN-50 turret was replaced by the heavier Martin 250CE equipped with two M2 0.50-in. machine guns. The RCAF's No. 6 Group (the Canadian component of Bomber Command) was the principal user of the B Xs, 430 of which were built between September 1943 and May 1945.

GERMAN FLAK DEFENCES

88mm FlaK 18/36/37

In April 1939 the Luftwaffe had 3,090 88mm/105mm heavy flak guns in service. The most numerous was the 88mm FlaK 18. Entering service in 1933, it was of fairly conventional design. The new 88mm weapon incorporated direct transmission of firing solutions from the fire director to the gun itself. A well-trained crew (initially consisting of ten men, but later reduced to seven) could fire up to 15 rounds a minute. The 19.8lb explosive shell had an effective ceiling of 26,000ft.

The next versions of the 88mm weapon to appear were the FlaK 36 and 37. Each had the same performance as the FlaK 18, but with some key changes. The FlaK 36 had

Flakzwilling 40/2

Code named *'Innsbruck'*, the twin-barrelled 128mm Flakzwilling was one of the best, largest and most effective heavy flak weapons of the war. Compared to the standard 88mm flak gun, the 128mm's powder charge was four times as large, reducing shell flight time by two-thirds. This in turn meant that gunners could engage fast-moving targets more effectively. Crewed by up to 12 men (usually the best gunners in the *Jagdwaffe*), the Flakzwilling 40/2 had a rate of fire of 24 rounds per minute.

a three-section barrel held together with an enveloping 'outer sleeve'. This modification meant that instead of replacing the whole barrel due to wear, only the worn section had to be swapped, thus saving time and steel. The FlaK 37 had an improved mounting, electrical data transmission system and an automatic fuse setter connected directly to the fire control predictor. The gun-laying system was known as 'follow the pointer', which not only made the crew's work simpler but also improved their accuracy. Thanks to its advanced electrical data transmission system, the FlaK 37 was used exclusively in the anti-aircraft role by the *Flakartillerie*.

88mm FlaK 41

Entering service in March 1943, the FlaK 41 represented a major redesign and was arguably the best heavy anti-aircraft gun of the war. Even before the conflict began, the Luftwaffe recognized the need for an improved gun with a higher ceiling and muzzle velocity. Rheinmetall-Borsig duly commenced development of such a weapon (based on the 88mm gun already in production), and prototypes were ready for testing in early 1941. The FlaK 41 boasted outstanding ballistic characteristics, effectively firing shells up to a ceiling of 35,000ft – better than the larger calibre 105mm gun, let alone previous 88mm weapons. With a muzzle velocity of 3,315ft per second, the FlaK 41's performance represented a 20 per cent increase in both effective engagement altitude and shell velocity. However, the new gun required an extra 220lbs of steel and aluminium in its construction and the FlaK 41 was continuously plagued by a number of technical problems even after it had entered service. By the end of 1942 just 48 examples had been produced, and only 556 reached the *Flakartillerie* by war's end.

105mm FlaK 38/39

Like the FlaK 41, the 105mm FlaK 38 and 39 were developed to meet any future high-altitude threat. Entering service just before the outbreak of war, the FlaK 38 had

FlaK 18 Shell

FlaK 18 fixed high explosive (HE) 88mm shell (right) fitted with a spring-wound mechanical time fuse. The shell weighed 31.69lbs and had a length of 36.69in. The 88mm HE round was clearly identified to those handling the shell by its distinctive yellow-coloured projectile.

FlaK 41 Shell

FlaK 41 HE 88mm projectile (far right) filled with Amatol 40/60 and fused with a Zt. ZS/30Fgl or AZ23/26 cap. Weighting 20lbs 1oz, the shell had a bursting charge consisting of 2.19lbs of TNT or Amatol 40/60. The AZ23/28 fuse cap could be adjusted for immediate action or a 0.1-second delay in detonation.

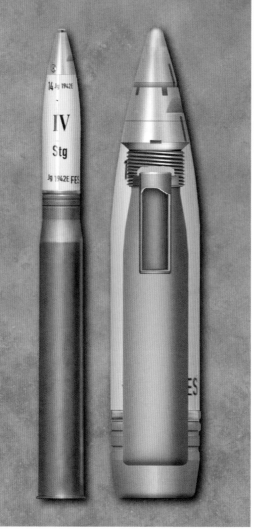

a powered ramming system and power-assisted gun laying, and was operated by a crew of nine. The FlaK 39 was similar in design, but incorporated an electrical data transmission system. Capable of firing 15 rounds a minute, the FlaK 38/39 had an effective ceiling of 31,000ft. Approximately 4,180 guns were produced during the war.

128mm FlaK 40

The 128mm FlaK 40 was the largest-calibre and most effective heavy flak gun deployed by the Luftwaffe. However, its 26ft length and weight of more than 28,000lbs meant it could only be used as a fixed-base weapon or when mounted to rail cars. Twin-barreled Flakzwilling 40/2s were designed to sit atop the massive concrete flak towers built to protect Berlin, Hamburg and Vienna. Firing a 57lb shell, the FlaK 40 had a ceiling of 35,000ft and a rate of fire of ten rounds per minute. The 128mm weapon was the most capable heavy flak gun of the war. Compared to 88mm and 105mm guns, the 128mm weapon averaged 3,000 rounds per aircraft shot down – half as many as the 105mm and less than one-fifth for the older 88mm FlaK 18 model. Just 1,125 FlaK 40s, including Flakzwilling 40/2s, were built.

ORDNANCE

In order to shoot down or damage a heavy bomber, a time-fused shell had to detonate within 30–80ft of the target – the exploding shell produced shrapnel of varying sizes, all of which could be deadly to a relatively lightly-armoured bomber. To improve the chances of hitting an aircraft with a damaging shell fragment, the Luftwaffe introduced the controlled-fragmentation round. Grooved cuts on the inside face of the shell casing produced a smaller pattern of fragments, but they were larger and more uniform in size. These rounds proved far more effective than the standard high-explosive shell.

In the final weeks of the war the Luftwaffe tested a projectile that had both a timed and contact fuse – this was christened a *Doppelzünder* (double effect) fuse by the Germans. During combat trails in April 1945, heavy flak batteries using experimental

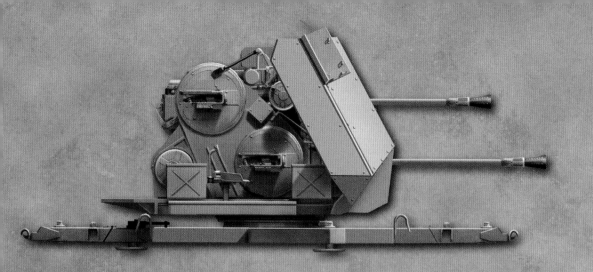

FlaK 43 Zwilling

By as early as 1941, Bomber Command reported light and medium flak to be effective 'up to at least 12,000ft, and possibly up to 16,000ft'. Because of the RAF's lower operating heights, light and medium flak was effectively employed throughout the war. In order to increase firepower, the *Flakwaffe* developed the 37mm

FlaK 43 Zwilling. Its twin-barrel configuration increased rate of fire to more than 250 rounds per minute, although operators complained that it was both top-heavy and too unwieldy to move with ease. Fortunately for RAF bomber crews, relatively few FlaK 43 Zwilling batteries were produced, with just 390 being in service in 1945.

Doppelzünder fuses brought down 13 aircraft. On average, only 370 rounds had been expended per victory, which compared very favourably with 4,500 rounds per aircraft for standard shells. The *Doppelzünder* fuse was a truly remarkable, and frightening, development.

The Luftwaffe also employed a vast number of captured weapons in the defence of the Reich. These included British 3in. and 3.7in. guns, French and Dutch 75mm weapons, Italian 90mm guns, Czech 7.5cm artillery pieces and Russian 7.62cm and 85mm guns. It is estimated that between 1939 and 1944, the Luftwaffe issued the *Flakartillerie* with 9,504 captured guns and close to 14 million rounds of ammunition.

LIGHT AND MEDIUM FLAK

Although light and medium flak batteries did not play a major role in the defence against the heavy bomber, they did make a contribution nevertheless – particularly when these aircraft carried out precision raids on key industrial targets. Any damaged bomber caught at low level would be engaged by a variety of weapons, mostly FlaK 30/38 20mm guns and FlaK 18/36/43 37mm weapons. British bombers like the Stirling and early variants of the Halifax, flying at between 12,000–15,000ft, were also vulnerable to light and medium flak. Operational reports by Bomber Command crews indicated that light flak was seen at altitudes up to 16,000ft.

KOMMANDOGERÄT 36/40

The brains of the flak battery was its gun director. Known as 'predictors' in Britain and 'directors' in the USA, they were called *Kommandogerät* (command equipment)

The *Kommandogerät* 40 was the brains of the flak battery, the one-and-a-half-ton director requiring 13 personnel to operate it. Normally attached to a four-gun battery, the KodoG 40 combined an optical range finder with a ballistic computer. This combination produced precise firing solutions for visible targets. (Author's Collection)

The FuMG 39T(C) *Würzburg D* gun-laying radar had a range of 25 miles. Introduced in 1941, it quickly became the Luftwaffe's standard gun-laying radar system for the entire war. More than 4,000 units were built by Telefunken. (Author's Collection)

in Germany. The standard system used at the beginning of the war was the KodoG 36. Combined with height and range finders, the one-and-half-ton KodoG 36 required 13 men to operate it. Information from the height and range finders was fed into the KodoG 36, as were values for temperature, drift, velocity and other factors, with the resulting calculation producing a future position for the incoming formation. This data – bearing, range and fuse setting – was sent directly to the guns via electrical cables. Unable to cope with manoeuvring targets, the KodoG 36 was superseded by the improved KodoG 40, which was capable of tracking a target in a steady turn. It was standard *Flakartillerie* practice to have four heavy guns connected to a single KodoG 36/40.

GUN-LAYING RADAR

British gunners would have a hard time hitting Luftwaffe bombers during the *Blitz* of 1940–41, due to their lack of an effective guidance system. Similarly, their counterparts in the *Flakartillerie* were virtually blind when it came to defending Germany at the start of Bomber Command's nocturnal campaign in the summer of 1940, flak units relying almost exclusively on RRH sound detectors for tracking information. It was patently obvious that a new night tracking system was needed, and this finally reached frontline units from the summer of 1941 in the form of the FuMG 39T(C) *Würzburg* gun-laying radar. This system was capable of providing flak and searchlight units with an effective means of targeting aircraft at night or when flying through cloud during daylight.

By December 1941 the improved FuMG 39T(D) had been introduced, and this quickly became the *Flakartillerie*'s standard gun-laying radar. In 1942 the *Funkmessgerat* 39 (FuMG 39) and

later, FuMG 41 radars also became available, and these supplanted the FuMG 39T(D). Perhaps the best *Würzburg*-based gun-laying system of them all was the FuMG 65 *Würzburg-Riese* (Giant *Würzburg*), based on the FuMG 39T(D). Featuring a considerably larger antenna and more powerful transmitter, it could provide direct gun-laying for flak batteries. It was too large for truck transportation, however, and had to be mounted on railway carriages instead – this version was designated the *Würzburg-Riese-E*, and 1,500 were built.

When operating in combination at night, the gun-laying radar and command equipment

The FuMG 65 *Würzburg-Riese*, known to Allied intelligence as the 'Würzburg Giant', was one of the most common air search radars used by the *Flakwaffe* during 1942–45. Weighing 11 metric tons, it was usually mounted in a static position. Range was 44 miles, with an azimuth accuracy of 0.2 degrees and an elevation accuracy 0.1 degrees. (Author's Collection)

(predictor) produced a reliable fire solution. Early *Würzburg* radars had a range of between 15 and 24 miles (the *Würzburg-Riese-E* could detect targets at distances of up to 43 miles) and an accuracy, under ideal conditions, of plus or minus 12 to 15 yards. When the *Flakartillerie* rapidly expanded in size from 1942, there were never enough radar systems to go around, leaving 5,560 RRH sound detectors in operation in 1944.

SEARCHLIGHTS AND SOUND DETECTORS

The standard method of aiming searchlights in the early years of the war was with RRH sound detectors, despite their accuracy being adversely affected by weather, humidity, the altitudes at which bombers flew and their crews routinely changing the pitch of their engines in order to confuse those manning the detectors.

One of the essential ingredients of the Reich flak defences were the *Scheinwerfer Regimenten* (searchlight batteries). At the beginning of the war, the most widely used searchlight was the 150cm *Flakscheinwerfer 37*, which was joined by the 200cm *Falkscheinwerfer 40* Master Light in 1942. Searchlight batteries played a major role assisting both flak and nightfighters, and if one or more lights caught a bomber, the resulting glare prevented its crew from dropping their ordnance with any kind of accuracy.

THE STRATEGIC SITUATION

Between 1933 and 1938, Germany's ground-based defence forces had undergone a manifold expansion. Despite some production delays, the Luftwaffe's *Flakartillerie* was considered the best-equipped force of its type in the world. In many ways, Germany was better prepared to meet any future bombing campaign than the British and French were at mounting one.

Hitler's insistence on a robust and well-equipped flak force led to one of the most grandiose construction projects of the war, namely the Air Defence Zone. Work commenced in June 1938, with the focus being on protecting the industrial Ruhr. Hundreds of flak guns were duly built, as were searchlights and RRH sound detectors. Despite the volume of weaponry allocated to it, the Air Defence Zone was never envisioned as being an impenetrable barrier. Instead, it was to act as a deterrent, designed to force enemy crews up to higher altitudes, and thus reduce the accuracy of their bombing.

By 1939, sites for 788 88mm or 105mm guns and 576 20mm or 37mm guns were ready for action. This number dramatically increased as the Third Reich found itself increasingly targeted around the clock by Allied heavy bombers. In January 1944 there were 20,625 flak guns (7,941 heavy and 12,684 light/medium weapons) and 6,880 searchlights defending Germany, with a goodly number of these to be found in the Ruhr Valley – the most heavily defended region in the embattled country.

In the early stages of the war the RAF bombing campaign was extraordinarily limited. As previously noted, three telling raids mounted in daylight against warships and their naval bases in December 1939 resulted in heavy losses of Wellington and

Blenheim IV bombers to both flak and fighters. Those that survived returned to their bases with varying degrees of damage. The attrition suffered on these raids shook Bomber Command's faith in daylight missions of this type, leaving them with two alternatives – switch to night bombing or develop a long-range escort fighter. The latter was never seriously considered, as many believed a defensive fighter like the Spitfire could not carry enough fuel. Nevertheless, 60 Spitfire IIA Long Range variants with a single 30-gallon tank fitted beneath its port wing saw limited service in the defence of RAF light bombers in 1941. They were not a success.

That left bomber crews having to rely on the cover of darkness. In the first quarter of 1941, the Luftwaffe estimated that the ratio of night raids to day raids by Bomber Command was 40–to–1. While the RAF's switch to night-bombing led to fewer losses, its effectiveness was questionable. Described as amateurish and incoherent, Bomber Command's early bomber offensive, between May 1940 and February 1942, failed to inflict any real damage. Conducting a precision night-bombing campaign was next to impossible with the aircraft and equipment it then had at its disposal. In August 1941 the Butt Report revealed that at best only ten to twenty per cent of bombers were dropping their loads within five miles of their intended targets. Add in the ten to thirty per cent of bombs that did not explode, and the success rate was dismal.

Despite the focus placed on them pre-war, German flak defences were barely any more effective. Like the RAF, the *Flakartillerie* had never intended to fight a night war in the air. The sound detectors used by the Luftwaffe to locate bombers at night quickly proved inadequate. And when a bomber was caught in a searchlight, the low rates of fire and accuracy achieved by the heavy guns remained poor. As with Bomber Command, the *Flakartillerie* had to adapt. By 1940, the Luftwaffe had organized a number of *Speerfeuerbatterien* 'barrage barrier' batteries designed to put up a box of flak over the protected target. Wasteful in ammunition, the intent was to force any bomber formation to abandon its run or disrupt the crews' aim. Not until the advent of gun-laying radar in 1941 did the flak arm improve its accuracy, which in turn boosted morale throughout the *Flakartillerie*. Its gunners now had the 'eyes' to see at night, and their results improved accordingly.

Between January and April 1941, flak batteries in the western occupied territories accounted for 115 of the 144 enemy aircraft destroyed. In Germany, during the same period, they destroyed 121 of the 144 enemy aircraft shot down. Although the flak arm was now dramatically improving its effectiveness, the same could not be said for the RAF's bombing campaign. The introduction of the Stirling and Halifax in late 1940 had finally given Bomber Command heavy bombers capable of carrying

Flak bursts and tracer fire from light flak guns greet an incoming RAF raid over Kiel. Attacking from lower altitudes at night, Bomber Command squadrons were often targeted by light and medium flak. The latter also inflicted a toll on Allied 'heavies' undertaking low-level precision-bombing raids, both during the day and at night. The RAF conducted a number of these operations in the Lancaster, including the famous Dams Raid on 16/17 May 1943. These missions typically suffered heavy losses, confirming that low-level attacks were not viable with heavy bombers. On 16/17 September 1943, eight Lancasters from No. 617 Sqn performed a low-level attack on the Dortmund–Ems Canal. Five aircraft were lost to flak, which prompted Bomber Command to suspend all future low-level raids by heavy bombers. (Author's Collection)

In the first few years of the war the *RRH* sound detector was the standard method for aiming searchlights and heavy flak guns. Its reliability, accuracy and range (which varied between three and seven miles) could be adversely affected by weather conditions, including humidity, aircraft flying at higher altitudes and ambient noise levels associated with combat. Primitive in nature, the sound detector was good at determining direction, but little else. (Author's Collection)

destructive loads. Slow production rates, however, had limited their impact. Furthermore, poor bombing accuracy at night remained a major problem. In an attempt to solve this, the Air Ministry decided to simply aim for a bigger target – German cities.

By early 1942 the fate of the RAF's strategic bombing campaign was being debated at the highest level. Bomber Command stood at a crossroads. Britain's industrial and manpower effort was fully stretched. Supporters of strategic bombing restated their old argument – 'the only way to win the war was to bomb Germany with such force as to cause the collapse of German morale and avoid a costly land invasion'. The German invasion of the Soviet Union in June 1941 had also changed the equation. Britain's only means of striking Germany directly, and thus helping the Soviet cause, was by bombing. Chief of the Air Staff Sir Charles Portal convinced Prime Minister Winston Churchill that with a large force of heavy bombers this objective could be achieved. While not fully convinced, Churchill agreed, leading to one of the most momentous decisions of the war.

On 14 February 1942, General Directive No. 5, subsequently known as the Area Bombing Directive, was issued to Bomber Command. German cities were now its primary objectives, targeting 'the morale of the enemy civil population and, in particular, of the industrial worker'.

Eight days later Bomber Command also received a new leader, Air Marshal Arthur Harris. With an almost religious faith in area bombing, he was equally enthusiastic in regard to the new Lancaster and its capabilities. Unfortunately for Harris, the force he inherited was the same size (469 night bombers) as it had been throughout much of 1941. The only difference was the presence of 29 Stirlings, 29 Halifaxes and four Lancasters.

America's entry into the war in December 1941 meant an increase in aid and assistance. It also eventually signalled the appearance of USAAF B-17s and B-24s at bases in England. Germany now faced two strategic air forces dedicated to its destruction. While the RAF and the USAAF agreed on the end result, they went about it in very different ways. The USAAF held strong in its belief that daylight 'precision' bombardment held the key to victory. While Eighth and Fifteenth Air Force bomb groups focused on targeting individual factories and other important sites during the day, the RAF was content to blast German cities to rubble at night.

Because cloud cover routinely blanketed most targets over western Europe, the USAAF was eventually forced to adopt the RAF's area bombing techniques, using H2X ground-mapping radar and other electronic navigating devices – by the autumn of 1943, the first H2X radar-equipped B-17Gs had entered service. The 'blind' or nonvisual method met with mixed results, with 42 per cent of bombs dropped during the winter of 1944–45 falling more than five miles from their intended target.

On 17 August 1942, the Eighth Air Force launched Mission No. 1. Escorted by RAF Spitfires, 12 B-17s attacked the Sotteville railway marshalling yards near Rouen. Bombing from 23,000ft, the mission was judged to have been a success. Crucially, none of the bombers were lost. During the second half of 1942 the Eighth Air Force grew in size to six bomb groups – four with B-17Fs and two with B-24Ds. By the end of 1942, 30 daylight missions (all against targets in occupied Europe, but not Germany itself) had been flown, with limited results. Losses were light and optimism was high. Most USAAF unit commanders downplayed the threat posed by flak, but not everyone was in agreement.

Streams of 37mm tracer fire concentrate at a single point. The Stirling's low ceiling made it particularly vulnerable to medium and light flak such as this. While the bomber's ceiling was officially listed as 17,000ft, it was often much lower due to maximum bomb and fuel loads, placing it well within range of the 37mm FlaK 36/37 guns. (Author's Collection)

1943 proved to be the pivotal year in the ETO, with the first major German defeats of the war altering the strategic balance. The Wehrmacht's 6th Army surrendered at Stalingrad in February, the *Afrika Korps* was defeated in North Africa in May and the Royal Navy and US Navy enjoyed their first notable victories against the U-boats in the Atlantic (43 U-boats were sunk in May alone). At last, the Allies had the initiative.

In January 1943 the Allied leaders issued the 'Casablanca Directive'. This document provided the foundation for the joint Allied air offensive, aimed directly at crippling Germany's industrial base. Detailed plans in support of the new strategy, however, did not appear for a further six months. By March of that year Bomber Command was capable of launching more than 400 aircraft (half of which were heavy bombers) at a time. At that point the Eighth Air Force was only just beginning to conduct missions with more than 100 bombers at a time, although it quickly ramped up operations. On 1 November 1943, the USAAF activated the Fifteenth Air Force. Operating out of Foggia, the Fifteenth gave the Allies its third strategic heavy bomber formation in the ETO.

For the Germans, the start of 1943 was greeted with a mix of confidence and worry. Up to that point the performance of the flak defences had seemed effective and robust, although the critical loss of men and materiel on the Eastern Front and in North Africa caused a nagging shortage of personnel in both the Luftwaffe and the Wehrmacht. This led directly to the mobilization of men and women, young and old, for duty in the *Flakartillerie*. Yet despite the growing personnel problems, 1943 witnessed a further increase in the number of guns and searchlights operating within the Reich. At the start of the new year, 659 heavy and 558 light flak batteries were located in Germany, and that number had jumped to 1,089 heavy and 738 light flak batteries by the middle of June. These totals would rise dramatically in the final two years of the conflict.

The bloodiest flak battles were yet to come, for by January 1943 Allied bombers had only dropped 6.5 per cent of the total tonnage of bombs expended on Germany during World War II.

NEXT PAGE

Principal targets attacked by Bomber Command in 1944–45

43

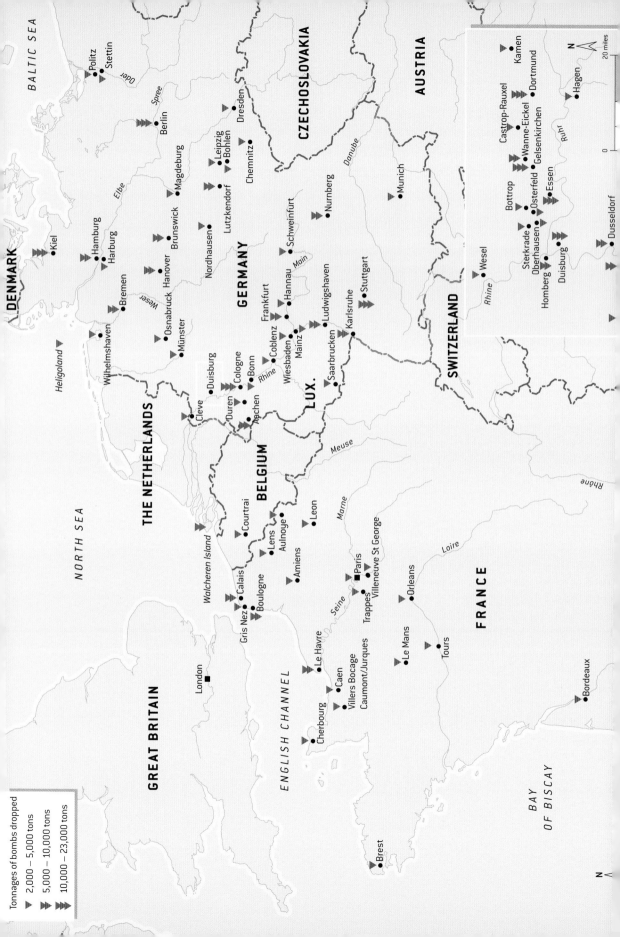

BALTIC SEA

DENMARK

Politz
Stettin
Oder

Spree
Berlin
Dresden

CZECHOSLOVAKIA

AUSTRIA

Kamen
Castrop-Rauxel
Dortmund
Wanne-Eickel
Gelsenkirchen
Hagen

Leipzig
Bohlen
Magdeburg
Chemnitz

N
20 miles
0

Bottrop
Osterfeld
Essen
Ruhr

Nordhausen
Lutzkendorf

Munich

Sterkrade
Oberhausen
Homberg
Duisburg

Schweinfurt
Nurnberg

Kiel
Hamburg
Harburg

Brunswick

GERMANY

Main
Wesel

Dusseldorf

Hanover

Frankfurt
Hannau
Ludwigshaven
Stuttgart

Wesel

Bremen
Osnabruck
Munster

Coblenz

Karlsruhe

Rhine

Heligoland

Weser

Wilhelmshaven

Duisburg
Cologne
Bonn

Wiesbaden
Mainz
Saarbrucken

SWITZERLAND

Rhine

NORTH SEA

THE NETHERLANDS

Cleve
Duren
Aachen

LUX.

Meuse

Rhone

Courtrai

BELGIUM

Leon
Marne

Walcheren Island

Lens
Aulnoye

Paris
Villeneuve St George

Calais
Boulogne

Amiens

Trappes

Loire

Orleans

FRANCE

Gris Nez

Seine

GREAT BRITAIN

London

ENGLISH CHANNEL

Le Havre
Caen
Villers Bocage
Caumont/Jurques

Le Mans
Tours

Cherbourg

Brest

BAY
OF BISCAY

Bordeaux

N

Tonnages of bombs dropped
▶ 2,000 – 5,000 tons
▶▶ 5,000 – 10,000 tons
▶▶▶ 10,000 – 23,000 tons

THE COMBATANTS

'It is essential to understand that flying a bomber required a good measure of brute physical strength.'
Max Hastings, author of *Bomber Command*

RAF BOMBER COMMAND AIRCREW

To fly a heavy four-engined bomber during World War II required a set of skills quite different from those of a fighter pilot. During training, pilots who showed outstanding reflexes and necessary skills to handle a Spitfire or Hurricane were generally sent to Fighter Command. Undoubtedly, the vast majority of recruits thought they would fly fighters, with few, if any, dreaming they would find themselves at the controls of an overloaded heavy bomber surrounded by the inky blackness of night, constant flak, probing searchlights and, more often than not, poor weather conditions. Despite the romantic image of the fearless fighter pilot, airmen knew there was no special temperament that gave one man the ability to handle a Spitfire and another a four-engined heavy bomber.

For the young student pilot, the type of aircraft he would eventually fly in the frontline was out of his control. When the choice was made, many were met with disappointment. One such individual was Canadian Murray Peden, who wrote in his autobiography, *A Thousand Shall Fall*, 'Thus, despite my frequently expressed preferences, my pleas, and my prayers, I was denied the chance to fly fighters.' Peden would fly Stirling Is and Fortress IIs in combat, receiving a DFC at the end of his tour.

No. 75 (NZ) Sqn's Sgt Don Whitehead and his all NCO crew photographed before takeoff from Newmarket, in Suffolk, on 24 April 1943. A mixed crew, hailing from Britain and New Zealand, they had all completed intensive training prior to coming together at an OTU. Surviving intensive operations throughout the Battle of the Ruhr in Bomber Command's most vulnerable heavy bomber, they are, from left to right, Rex Jamieson RNZAF (rear gunner), Maurice Parker RNZAF (bomb aimer), Charlie Parker RNZAF (wireless operator), George Stokes RAFVR (mid-upper gunner), Hugh McLellan RAFVR (flight engineer), Don Whitehead RNZAF (pilot) and Peter Dobson RNZAF (navigator). (Gray Cameron)

In many ways, flying a heavy bomber at night on instruments required far more skill than flying a Spitfire during the day on a short interception or escort mission.

By 1942, most of the pre-war generation of aircrew had been killed, wounded, captured or promoted to non-operational duties. Thanks to the British Commonwealth Air Training Plan that commenced in December 1939, aircrew from Britain, Canada, Australia, New Zealand and South Africa had been available to replace them. The need for such recruits only increased with the delivery of more and more Stirling, Halifax and Lancaster heavy bombers to the RAF, each of which had a seven-man crew – pilot, flight engineer, navigator, bombardier/nose gunner, wireless operator, mid-upper gunner and rear gunner. Crew training for a heavy bomber was an expensive, time-consuming and dangerous endeavour. Hundreds of schools, airfields and training depots were established to take on this war-winning task in Britain, Canada, New Zealand, South Africa, Rhodesia and Australia.

The long process of training began with the aircrew selection board. Facing two or three officers, a nervous volunteer had only moments to impress and make his case – there were no second chances. For the successful candidate, the long assembly-line process of aircrew training began shortly thereafter. For overseas volunteers, the next step was the local manning depot or, in the case of British recruits, the RAF Volunteer Reserve (RAFVR). More interviews followed, as did lectures, tests and countless hours of drills. One or two hours were also spent in the Link Trainer, the 1940s' version of today's flight simulator.

The Link Trainer was used to introduce the would-be pilot to the art of instrument flying. If he was unable to master the craft at this early stage, he soon found himself with a new vocation – flight engineer, bombardier, navigator, wireless operator or air gunner. For those who survived the Link Trainer experience, Elementary Flying Training School was next.

Student pilots began with ten months of basic flight training. Starting on single-engined de Havilland Tiger Moth biplanes, trainees accumulated approximately 78 hours of flight time before moving onto Service Flying Training School (SFTS). It was at this point the young recruit learned his fate. Those streamed for fighters moved onto the North American Harvard or Yale (the latter was a fixed undercarriage version of the Harvard) advanced trainers, while students selected for multi-engined aircraft found themselves flying Avro Ansons, Airspeed Oxfords or Cessna Cranes. Arguably the hardest part of the SFTS course was Beam Approach Training, which saw student pilots having to master a radio-based blind-landing system in order to successfully land at night. After logging 120 hours (including 20 hours of night flying, much of this accrued during Beam Approach Training flights) on twin-engined types, the cadet was finally awarded his wings.

Pilots took the longest to train, with the remaining bomber crewmen completing shorter courses of varying lengths – navigators took 58 weeks, wireless operators 22 weeks and air gunners between seven and eighteen weeks.

When pilots and crewmen trained overseas arrived in Britain, they were assigned to Advanced Flying Units. Here, they learned to fly in fickle local weather and blackout conditions. Next stop was the Operational Training Unit (OTU), where future frontline crews were formed and the process of working together began. Flying well-worn Wellington bombers, each crew spent ten weeks grappling with long-range navigation, high-level bombing and aerial gunnery. Surprisingly, only a third of the flights with the OTU were undertaken at night. By the end of OTU course pilots would have flown, on average, 26 hours dual and close to 60 hours as captain.

The final step prior to reaching an operational squadron was the Heavy Conversion Unit (HCU), where the new 'sprog' crews would learn to fly the heavy bomber they would use operationally. To the disappointment of many, the aircraft that equipped the HCUs were 'de-rated', which meant that opening the throttle to full power was forbidden for fear of literally blowing up the bomber's engines. After 30 hours of flight time at the HCU, crews were considered ready for squadron assignment. Despite all the training they had received, many new crews found flying a fully armed and fuelled four-engined bomber at night a difficult task to master. Accidents were frequent, as were fatalities. In late 1943 the attrition rate reached such high levels that Bomber Command created 'Finishing Schools', which gave crews additional flying time between leaving an HCU and joining an operational squadron.

Bomber Command aircrew were young, typically aged between 18 and 22. Although the training they received was thorough from a technical standpoint, nothing could really prepare them for the cold, harsh realities of war. Serving in an operational squadron on a bomber station could be a particularly grim business. New crews were usually given the oldest and most vice-ridden aircraft in the unit upon their arrival. By 1944, the best crews in Bomber Command were assigned to the elite Pathfinder Force and Mosquito squadrons. Being part of the 'Main Force' held no special providence, and had in fact become a term of condescension. But in the end, it did not matter. Experienced crews were just as likely to get shot down as novice ones. It was all a matter of luck. The nightly threat of flak and fighters exacted a heavy toll on Bomber Command, with a sustained mission loss rate of 3.3 to 5 per cent meaning that no aircrew would survive a standard 25-mission tour.

Forced to undertake a night-bombing campaign with aircraft designed for daylight operations, Bomber Command endured a casualty rate of more than 61 per cent, with 44 per cent being killed. Approximately 85 per cent of the casualties were suffered on operations, with the remaining 15 per cent lost in training and other non-operational accidents.

USAAF BOMBER AIRCREW

Even before war had engulfed Europe, the United States was quietly making moves to expand its armed forces. The USAAC had laid plans to expand aircrew training to 1,200 pilots a year by 1941, and this figure was later revised upwards to 7,000 a year and again to 30,000 in 1941. The US government also knew that it was only a matter of time before the country was at war with Germany. Secret meetings between senior US and British staff officers in January and March 1941 established a course of action whereby American warships, troops and aircraft would be committed to the campaign against the Axis powers in the European theatre.

Aircrew training for the USAAF (as the USAAC was renamed on 20 June 1941) essentially followed the same pattern as for the RAF – Primary Flying School, Basic Flying School, Advanced Flying Training and Transition Flying Training. The first step, however, was different. Would-be aircrew initially undertook a five-week basic military course. Here, aviation cadets went through a five-week regime that included exhaustive physical, psychological and mental tests to determine their suitability for the flying programme, and to determine which speciality was best for them.

America's full entry into the war on 7 December 1941 saw the rapid expansion of the USAAF and President Franklin D. Roosevelt's support for the acquisition of heavy bombers. It was a formidable training challenge. The new B-17 and B-24 required a crew of ten men – two-thirds larger than the standard crew for the B-18 and North American B-25 Mitchell medium bombers. It was estimated that more than 500 separate skills were required to execute a 'routine' bombing mission. The Commanding General of the newly renamed USAAF was fully aware of this Lt Gen 'Hap' Arnold stating in 1942 that 'this is an age of specialization. No rational man can hope to know everything about his profession'.

American bombers also adopted the two-pilot system (British bombers had one pilot, with a flight engineer to assist), which meant twice as many aviators had to be trained. By 1944, the minimum number of hours required to produce a qualified pilot was as follows – Primary, 60 hours; Basic, 70 hours; Advanced, 75 hours. Those chosen for multi-engined types accumulated 70 hours flying twin-engined trainer like the Beechcraft AT-7 Navigator, AT-10 Wichita and AT-11 Kansan and the Cessna AT-17 Bobcat. Based on their performance in these types, trainees were then selected for medium or heavy bombers, transports or twin-engined fighters.

Wearing their newly minted silver pilot's wings, aviators earmarked for heavy bombers commenced learning how to fly the type. During Transition Flying Training they received 105 hours of four-engined training, after which pilots reported to their unit training group. There, they would hone their formation flying, navigation and bombing skills prior to being posted to an operational squadron.

Navigator and bombardier training also required a great deal of specialization and time. In 1942, navigator cadets received 403 hours of ground school and 100 hours in the air during a course that lasted 15 weeks. Bombardier training was shorter, as the early demand for crews meant that courses had to be cut to just nine weeks. Three-quarters of the training consisted of ground classes in theory, bombsights and procedures, with bombardiers also honing their skills with the A-2 bombing simulator prior to taking to the air. After dropping between 120 and 145 practice bombs during qualification and 55 to 80 during the tactical training phase, the bombardier was considered ready. Both navigators and bombardiers also initially received some gunnery school training in the use of the flexibly-mounted 0.30-in. or 0.50-in. weapons. However, by mid-1942, the gunnery schools were so jammed with new recruits that many bombardiers and navigators arrived in England having never previously fired a weapon.

Gunners received the least amount of training, spending just six weeks studying their weapons, shell ballistics, turret operation and maintenance. Live firing included shooting at a moving target while on the ground, firing at ground targets from the air and working with towed targets.

Early in the war, the rapid expansion of the USAAF and the demand for new personnel to man recently formed squadrons resulted in far too many poorly trained crews. To address the problem, the USAAF adopted the RAF use of Finishing Schools and set up its own OTUs.

Well-trained aircrew were not the only personnel needed for combat. To get a single heavy bomber into the air required a small army of men. The B-17 and B-24 consisted of as many as 12,000 individual parts, and many of these needed replacement at some stage due to wear and tear or battle damage (the latter caused primarily by flak). A typical heavy bomb group (equipped with either B-17s or B-24s) was comprised of a group Headquarters with 25 officers, one warrant officer and 57 enlisted men, and four squadrons of 12 aircraft each. Each of the squadrons was manned by 67 officers and 360 enlisted air- and groundcrew. The total complement for one bomb group was 48 combat crews, consisting of 293 officers, one warrant officer, 1,487 enlisted men and 48 aircraft.

The instruction of enlisted men for ground duty was the USAAF's largest single training endeavour. No fewer than 34 separate skills were required, and 80 different types of course were taught, including communications (radio, radar, telegraph, telephone), aircraft maintenance and repair, armament and equipment, meteorological, photography, motor transport and Link Trainer operation. By the end of the war an astonishing 670,000 aircraft maintenance specialists had been trained – the equivalent of 44 infantry divisions' worth of troops.

Wearing newly issued flak vests, Capt Leonard Cox (right) and his unidentified co-pilot pose in front of B-17F 42-29921 *OKLAHOMA OKIE* of the 324th BS/91st BG at Bassingbourn, in Cambridgeshire, on 16 June 1943. These early vests, grimly nicknamed 'flak suits', were made by the Wilkinson Sword Company and consisted of heavy canvas covered with overlapping two-inch squares of 20-gauge manganese steel. The vest's job was to protect the wearer's chest and back from low-velocity shrapnel, and their belated issuing to all crews was a tacit admission by the USAAF that flak was here to stay. Between May and December 1943, 42-29921 flew 34 missions and suffered flak damage listed as category A (repairable on base) on eight occasions. The aircraft was eventually shot down during a mission to Cognac, in southwest France, on 31 December 1943, 42-29921 being one of 25 bombers lost to flak that day. (Author's Collection)

Keeping serviceability rates at a high level put a great strain on groundcrews. Every flak hole, no matter how small, had to be patched. The following quote from the *Official World War II Guide to the Army Air Force*, published in 1944, reveals how much time and energy was spent on repairing damaged aircraft. It should also be noted that the vast majority of the damaged aircraft would be heavy bombers, as escort fighters rarely survived substantial flak damage:

> As an illustration of the demands of wartime maintenance, consider one hypothetical daylight bombing attack against a well defended target by a force of 150 bombers and 75 escort fighters. A fair assumption of losses would be: ten planes lost over enemy territory; six forced to land in locations away from their bases; 25 extensively damaged; 50 moderately damaged; 25 with minor damage and 109 unscathed. The six force-landings would require about 7,200 man-hours of maintenance; the 25 extensive damage would average about 450 man-hours each, making a total of 11,250 man-hours; the 50 moderately damaged, at an average of 300 man-hours, would require 15,000 man-hours; and the slightly damaged, averaging 150 man-hours, would total 3,750 man-hours. Total maintenance required for repairs alone (not service) would be 37,200 man-hours, or a 48-hour work week for 775 men.

Flakwaffe personnel man a British-built Vickers Model 1931 75mm anti-aircraft gun. Thousands of captured enemy anti-aircraft guns were pressed into German service during the war. After the defeat of Holland in May 1940, the Germans seized 90 stored Model 1931s and re-designated them 75mm Flak M 35(h)s – this particular weapon is almost certainly one of those guns. (Author's Collection)

Bomber crews faced myriad dangers – flak, fighters, collision, accidents, being hit by falling bombs and poor weather. Even without the enemy trying to shoot aircraft down, flying itself was not a safe pursuit as fighter and bombers were continually the subject of mechanical or structural failure. The safety of the crew depended on the reliability of the very thing they came to love, their aeroplane. In the end, the security of a bomber crew was inexorably linked to the efficiency of the groundcrews, and not to direct enemy action.

FLAKARTILLERIE

Germany's preparation for war in Europe devoted a great deal of resources to the deployment of anti-aircraft artillery. With Hitler as its most ardent supporter, the *Flakartillerie* was well supplied with guns, ammunition and qualified personnel. Responsibility for the flak defences of cities and industrial targets had been given to the Luftwaffe upon its formation in February 1935, which differed from how anti-aircraft artillery assets were controlled in Britain and the USA, where they were assigned to the army. The Wehrmacht and Kriegsmarine had their own flak units, but they were much smaller and controlled less than a quarter of the weapons available to the Luftwaffe.

Prior to the outbreak of war, the Luftwaffe had established *Flakartillerieschules* (Flak Schools) at Rerik and Stolpmunde with a third being created at Barth during the conflict. The introduction of radar also saw the establishment of two special *Luftkriegsschule* (training centres) in Berlin and Dresden.

A civilian-registered Junkers W 34 floatplane tows a flak target drogue during a live-firing training exercise off the Baltic coast for *Flakartillerie* personnel in the mid-1930s. By 1944 live fire training such as this had been drastically cut back due to the shortage of aviation fuel and ammunition and the transfer of most *Flakwaffe* instructors to infantry units on the Eastern Front. (Author's Collection)

Like aircrew training, preparing gunners for duty in the *Flakartillerie* required that they be taught a complex series of skills. Gun handling, ballistics, command and control, detection, acquisition and ranging of targets, and the production of a fire solution, all required precision and flawless team work. At the beginning of the war most flak crewmen were university students with a background in electrical or mechanical engineering, or something similar. By 1940 there were 528,000 men serving in the flak arm. Like the remaining personnel in the German armed forces, they were fit, motivated and well trained.

Preparing a flak crewman for war took far less time and expense than preparing airmen to man a heavy bomber. After completing basic, intermediate and advanced flak training, gunners undertook periodic live-firing training exercises at one of the 29 flak training sites located on the Baltic, Atlantic and Mediterranean coasts. Compared to Allied flak forces, the *Flakwaffe* (which was created on 12 January 1942 as part of the *Flakartillerie*) had a threefold responsibility – defence of cities and industry, mobile defences for ground forces and direct fire and artillery support against tanks and fortifications. This created a unique training regime, and one that would come under great strain as the Allied bombing campaign grew in both size and tempo.

The highest headquarters formation in the *Flakwaffe* was the *Flakkorps*. The latter was described in the following terms by a US Army intelligence report from 1943:

> The *Flakkorps* is a wartime organization, and constitutes an operational reserve of the commander in chief of the German Air Force. It combines great mobility with heavy firepower. It can be employed in conjunction with spearheads composed of armored and motorized forces, and with non-motorized troops in forcing river crossings and attacking fortified positions. It can also be deployed as highly mobile artillery to support tank attacks

Ammunition fuse setters carry out their critically important task on 88mm shells moments before they are loaded into the breech and fired. With each of these shells weighing 31lb 11oz, being an ammunition handler for an 88mm battery was physically taxing work. By the autumn of 1944 the ranks of the *Flakwaffe* had been bolstered by 98,000 'volunteer' and PoW ammunition handlers. (Author's Collection)

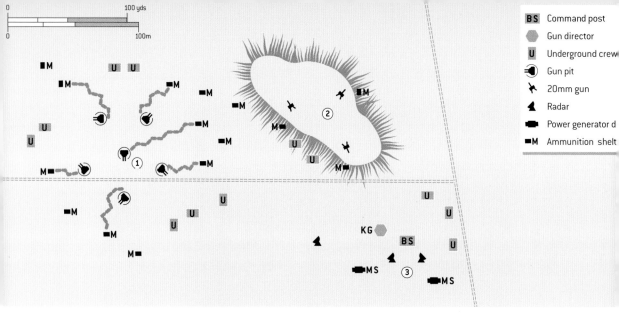

Legend:
- **BS** Command post
- Gun director
- **U** Underground crew
- Gun pit
- 20mm gun
- Radar
- Power generator d
- **M** Ammunition shelt

By 1943 the standard heavy flak battery had been increased in size to six guns. A typical site was approximately 1,000ft long and 400ft deep. The heavy gun battery (1) included six gun pits, with trenches connecting the weapons to their associated ammunition shelters (M) and underground crew shelters (U). Protection against low-flying aircraft conducting strafing attacks was provided by three 20mm gun batteries (2), usually sited on higher ground when available. The battery fire control centre (3) included the command post (BS – *Befehlsstand*), two radars, a gun director (KG – *Kommandogerät*) and two dugouts for power generator trailers (MS – *Maschinensatz Schuppen*).

As noted, the *Flakkorps* was fully motorized and operated closely with field armies. It usually consisted of between two and four *Flak Divisonen*, which could be either static or motorized. The static divisions (home defence), which came under the control of the local *Luftgau* (administrative and supply organizations of the Luftwaffe) headquarters, comprised two or more *Brigaden* (brigades), each with two or more *Regimenter* (regiments). A *Regimenter* normally consisted of between four and six *Abteilungen* (battalions) for static defence. At the beginning of 1945, the *Flakwaffe*'s strength stood at seven *Flakkorps*, 29 *Divisonen*, 13 *Brigaden* and 160 *Regimenter*.

The basic flak unit was the *Abteilung*, and it came in four main types – *Schwere* (heavy), *Leichte* (light), *Gemischte* (both heavy and light) and *Scheinwerfer* (searchlight).

By 1943 the *Flakwaffe* had entered a period of crisis. As the Allied bomber offensive began to expand in respect of the number of aircraft involved and the volume of targets being hit, the *Flakwaffe* was also forced to rapidly increase in size. However, heavy losses suffered by the Wehrmacht on all fronts during the early months of 1943 created a critical shortage of able-bodied men. Acting as a giant reserve, large numbers of *Flakwaffe* personnel were transferred to Wehrmacht units to serve as infantrymen or in the artillery. In their place came a mixed bag of men and women from various sources. In the desperate search for replacements, the Luftwaffe left no stone unturned. This meant all men aged between 16 and 65 were now eligible for service with the *Flakwaffe*.

By August 1943 the Luftwaffe had received more guns and equipment than it could possibly operate with its existing personnel. To address the demand *Reichsmarschall* Hermann Göring, Supreme Commander of the Luftwaffe, ordered the formation of *Flak Wehrmanner* (Home Guard) units consisting of factory and office workers. Equipped with a mix of older flak weapons and captured guns, the *Flak Wehrmanner* personnel worked at their civilian jobs during the day and trained at night. August 1943 also saw Hitler order the establishment of 250 additional flak batteries to be manned by the *Reich Arbeit Dienst* (Reich Labour Service), its personnel receiving three months of specialized training. Between September 1943 and February 1944, the number of flak batteries manned by *Reich Arbeit Dienst* draftees increased to 300.

In another development in August 1943, the Luftwaffe had begun drafting young men from German secondary schools to serve as Luftwaffe *Helfren* (air force

Recently recruited *Flakwaffe* gunners practise on the Baltic coast. In the static position, as seen here, the normal complement for an 88mm gun was ten men, as follows – a gun commander, a layer of elevation, a layer of line traversing, a loader, two fuse setters and four ammunition handlers. (Author's Collection)

auxiliaries). These 15–16-year-old boys would ultimately perform a number of roles that saw them manning flak batteries and searchlights, ensuring the supply of ammunition and serving in communications. By the end of May 1944 38,000 young men were ready for service, despite them having received only minimal training. This usually lasted about eight weeks, and was followed by 'on the job' instruction at their assigned gun battery.

In addition to the mobilization of young and older men, young women were also drafted into the *Flak Kampfhelferinnen* (fighting helpers). These women found employment in observation posts, fixed radar sites and barrage balloon, searchlight and gun batteries. During 1943 approximately 116,000 young women replaced regular Luftwaffe gunners in the defence of the Reich. In the last year of the war the severity of the personnel crisis led to the formation of all-female flak batteries. By April 1945 ten such batteries had been deployed in the defence of Berlin. Volunteer troops from Italy and Hungary also served in the *Flakwaffe*, while Soviet prisoners of war (PoW) were used for the various physical tasks associated with keeping the heavy guns operational.

As the demand for personnel increased, the amount of training was cut. In early 1944 new radar operators received six to eight weeks of training, and this had been slashed to just three or four weeks by December. Accuracy, fire discipline and the overall effectiveness of heavy flak batteries decreased as a result.

In October 1944 the *Flakwaffe* personnel crisis was reflected in the make-up of 14. *Flak Division*, which was responsible for the defence of the vitally important Leuna synthetic oil refinery in central Germany. Of the 62,500 personnel of all ranks serving with this unit, just 28,000 were Luftwaffe regulars. The rest was made up of 18,000 *Reichs Arbeit Dienst*, 6,000 Luftwaffe-*Helfren,* 3,050 *Flak Kampfhelferinnen* and 900 Italian and Hungarian volunteers. It had also been allocated more than 3,600 Soviet PoWs.

Both the *Jagdwaffe* and the *Flakwaffe* relied on the successful detection and tracking of approaching raids in order to inflict the highest number of casualties on Allied heavy bombers. This photograph shows the inside of a Luftwaffe Fighter Control Centre, with plots on the movement of friendly and hostile aircraft being projected on the rear of the screen by some 40 Luftwaffe *Helfren* using small light projectors. Sat in front of the screen was the fighter divisional operations officer, along with his fighter controllers and flak liaison officers. (Author's Collection)

SIR ARTHUR T. 'BOMBER' HARRIS

Born on 13 April 1892 in Cheltenham, Gloucestershire, Arthur Harris was the son of a civil servant. In 1910 he emigrated to Southern Rhodesia, where he worked as a miner, coach driver and farmer. When World War I broke out he joined the 1st Rhodesia Regiment and fought against the Germans in South-West Africa. When the enemy was defeated Harris returned to farming, before heading to England in October 1915 and joining the Royal Flying Corps. Quickly learning to fly, he was promoted to flying officer on 29 January 1916 and duly served on the home front and in France, flying both Sopwith 1½ Strutters and Sopwith Camels with No. 45 Sqn. Harris claimed five victories with this unit on the Western Front, prior to being posted back to England to undertake Home Defence duties with No. 44 Sqn. He was awarded the Air Force Cross for his success in action, finishing the war with the rank of major.

Harris remained in the newly formed RAF post-war, seeing further combat during the 1920s in India, Mesopotamia and Persia. He earned his nickname 'Bomber' while trying to keep North West Frontier tribesman in check during his time in India. Harris also kept down uprisings in Mesopotamia through bombing. In 1927–29 he attended the Army Staff College at Camberley, in Surrey, after which he commanded a flying-boat squadron. In June 1933 Harris was promoted to group captain, and from 1934 to 1937 he was the Deputy Director of Plans in the Air Ministry. Promoted to air commodore in July 1937, he went on to command No. 4 (Bomber) Group from 1938. In September 1939 Harris was promoted to air vice marshal and given command of No. 5 Group. In November 1940 he was made Deputy Chief of the Air Staff and promoted to the acting rank of Air Marshal on 1 June 1941.

In August 1941 the Butt Report revealed that in 1940–41 just one in three RAF bombers had dropped their ordnance within five miles of their target during combat operations. With Bomber Command in crisis, the Air Ministry made the decision on 14 February 1942 to make German cities the primary objectives, targeting 'the morale of the enemy civil population and, in particular, of the industrial worker' through area bombing. With the new policy came a new leader. Just eight days after the new directive, Air Chief Marshal Arthur Harris was appointed C-in-C of Bomber Command. While Harris did not set bombing policy, he was an enthusiastic disciple. Indeed, in one of his most famous quotes of the war, he stated, 'There are a lot of people who say that bombing cannot win the war. My reply to that is that it has never been tried yet.' Harris would lead Bomber Command through to war's end, his name forever being linked with the Allies' controversial 'area bombing' campaign.

Promoted to Marshal of the Royal Air Force on 1 January 1946, Harris retired shortly thereafter and emigrated to South Africa in 1948. He returned to England three years later and eventually passed away on 5 April 1984.

Air Chief Marshal Sir Arthur T. 'Bomber' Harris (Author's Collection)

WALTHER VON AXTHELM

In January 1942 Hitler committed a large portion of the Wehrmacht's overall budget to anti-aircraft defences. At the same time he appointed General Walther von Axthelm as the *General der Flakartillerie* (Inspector of Anti-Aircraft Artillery).

Born in the town of Hersbruck, near Nuremburg, on 23 December 1893, von Axthelm joined the Royal Bavarian Army in 1913. Upon the outbreak of World War I he was transferred to the 8th Bavarian Field Artillery Regiment. Post-war, von Axthelm joined the 100,000-strong *Reichswehr* and served in a number of command and staff roles. In October 1932 he was transferred to the Reich Ministry of Defence in Berlin, and seven months later von Axthelm became the RLM's inspector general of the air defence force. Transferring to the Luftwaffe on 1 April 1935, he was closely mentored by Oberstleutnant Günther Rüdel, commander of *Flakartillerie* prior to the outbreak of World War II.

On 31 May 1940, von Axthelm was appointed commander of the *Flak-Brigade* I during the invasion of France. It was following the commencement of Operation *Barbarossa* in June 1941 that he came to the attention of Göring and the Luftwaffe leadership. Given command of *Flakkorps* I, his forces would claim approximately 300 aircraft and 3,000 armoured vehicles destroyed in just three months of combat in the East. For his performance, General von Axthelm received the *Ritterkreuz* (Knight's Cross). As a proven combat leader, and with extensive experience as a staff officer and tactical planner, von Axthelm was the perfect choice to lead the *Flakwaffe* upon its creation on 12 January 1942.

In this capacity, he played a decisive role in the decision of 1 September 1942 to resume work on anti-aircraft missiles. In April 1943, he also took over the position of inspector for *Flakzielgerät 76*, the V1 flying-bomb programme. Ironically, the V1 and anti-aircraft missile programmes ultimately had a detrimental effect on the *Flakwaffe*, for Hitler viewed the V1 and follow-on V2 as the perfect weapons to strike back at the Allies in response to their round-the-clock bombing campaign. As such, priority was given to these programmes, with the *Flakwaffe* instructed to make its best troops available to man the launch sites. A large number of officers and men from the flak arm were duly reassigned, thus exacerbating the personnel shortages already afflicting the *Flakwaffe*. The vengeance weapons also wasted thousands of tons of high explosives, with the V1s alone consuming more than 18,700,000lbs of Amatol (a mixture of TNT and ammonium nitrate) at a time when the *Flakwaffe* was suffering shortages of ammunition.

Von Axthelm was a loyal officer to the very end. By autumn 1944, the Luftwaffe's fighter arm no longer posed any real threat to the daylight bombing campaign in particular. Flak batteries would now have to provide the primary defence of the Third Reich. Despite serious manpower and ammunition shortages, von Axthelm continued to extol his troops in what he must have known was a hopeless fight. In December 1944, von Axthelm's New Year's message to the men and women of the flak arm revealed his state of mind:

> Men and women of the flak, the year 1944 has imposed heavy blows and trials on our people. We have succeeded in getting through them. Men and women of the flak, in the coming year, by day and night, with every shot at the enemy's aircraft think of the murdered women and children, the razed and destroyed cities and villages, the demolished cultural sites of our people. And in close cooperation with our fighters, with unsurpassed zeal, the never-tiring energy and commitment to duty will allow us to achieve our goal — the breaking of the enemy air terror.

Von Axthelm surrendered to American troops in May 1945 and was interned until 1947. He passed away on 6 January 1972.

General Walther von Axthelm (Public Domain)

COMBAT

'Flak, always a major cause of loss and damage, has steadily increased in relative importance to become the greatest single combat hazard in present-day operations.'
An Evaluation of Defensive Measures Taken to Protect Heavy Bombers from Loss and Damage. *Operational Analysis Section, November 1944*

At the beginning of 1942, the flak defences of the Reich and the Western Front totalled 866 heavy and 621 light gun batteries, as well as 273 searchlights batteries – an increase of 27, 13 and 23 per cent, respectively, on January 1941. As the flak forces increased, Bomber Command's strength seemed to stall. The high losses experienced during the second half of 1941 had led Prime Minister Winston Churchill to order the bomber force to be conserved. This duly meant that between 10 November 1941 and 22 February 1942 Bomber Command flew missions on just 54 nights, with the attacking strike force exceeding 200 aircraft on only four occasions.

On 30/31 May 1942 Bomber Command launched Operation *Millennium* – the first 'thousand-bomber raid' of the war. Drawing on all available resources, it managed to assemble 1,047 aircraft, including large numbers from OTUs, Training Command squadrons and HCUs. *Millennium* also represented the greatest number of heavy bombers used to attack a German city to date, with 131 Halifaxes, 88 Stirlings and 73 Lancasters being involved. Their target was Cologne, the third largest city in Germany. With the assistance of a full moon, 868 aircraft bombed the main target, causing a great deal of destruction. A total of 1,455 tons of bombs were dropped on the city, killing 486, injuring 55,027 and destroying 18,432 buildings.

The raid introduced a major innovation known as the 'bomber stream'. During an attack by 234 bombers on the city of Lübeck on 28/29 March 1942 (the first major raid following the issuing of 'area bombing' General Directive No. 5 on 14 February 1942), it had taken two hours for all of the aircraft involved to pass over the target area. This was seen as quite an achievement at the time. The new 'bomber stream' employed over Cologne allotted just 90 minutes for 1,000 aircraft to bomb the city. By flying a common route at the same speed, each individual bomber was allotted a height band and time slot over the target. This tactic was designed to swamp both Luftwaffe nightfighters and flak defences, which it duly did.

Overwhelmed by the size of the 'bomber stream', flak and searchlight batteries had to concentrate on individual targets, rather than employing their preferred barrier fire procedure. The RAF lost 41 bombers that night, with 22 being downed over the target – 16 by flak, four to fighters and two in a mid-air collision. A further 85 bombers were damaged by flak.

The Cologne operation was followed by two more 'thousand-bomber raids', with Essen being targeted on 1–2 June and Bremen on 25–26 June. The raid on Essen caused little damage, with just 11 houses destroyed, but the Bremen attack was more successful, with 572 dwellings being destroyed. Total losses for both missions amounted to 79 bombers. These three raids proved a major turning point in the strategic bombing of Germany. A clear message had been sent – Germany's largest cities were marked for destruction. In the wake of the attack on Cologne, Hitler publicly chided Göring for neglecting the city's flak defences, as Anthony Read noted in his book *The Devil's Disciples*:

> The Cologne raid was another nail in Göring's coffin. Hitler blamed him personally for his failure to protect the Reich, complaining to his adjutant, Nicolaus von Below, the Luftwaffe had never given the flak [arm] the attention it needed. 'This was the first time I had heard him criticize Göring', von Below wrote later. 'Hitler never regained absolute confidence in the *Reichsmarschall*.'

Despite the handful of 'thousand-bomber raids' in 1942, the Allied heavy bombing campaign against the Third Reich did not really start in earnest until January 1943. On the 27th of that month the Eighth Air Force mounted its first attack on a target in Germany when 64 B-17s were sent to attack the U-boat construction yards at Vegesack, on the Weser, near the port city of Bremen. Cloud cover over the target forced the formation to bomb Wilhelmshaven instead. The latter was also covered in cloud and a German smoke screen, however, resulting in just 53 B-17s dropping their bombs blindly from 25,000ft. That night, the RAF sent 157 heavy bombers – 124 Lancasters and 33 Halifaxes – to the city of Düsseldorf. This was the first time both USAAF and RAF heavy bomber formations had struck Germany within hours of each other, and these raids marked the start of the Allied 'round the clock' bombing campaign.

The growing number of RAF and American heavy bombers now being seen in German skies placed the Luftwaffe in a precarious position. Facing both night attacks on cities and daylight raids on industrial targets, hard choices had to be made as to where the increasingly thinly spread flak defences should be concentrated.

OVERLEAF

On 1 January 1945 Bomber Command sent 102 Lancasters and two Mosquitoes on a daylight raid to the Dortmund–Ems Canal near Ladbergen. Two Lancasters were lost to flak, one of which was PD377/WS-U of No. 9 Sqn. Moments after its bomb load had been released, the aircraft, flown by Flg Off R. F. H. Denton, was hit by flak and set on fire. Seeing the mid-upper turret engulfed in flames, wireless operator Flt Sgt George Thompson plunged through the smoke and flames and dragged the gunner to safety. Diving back into the inferno, Thompson then pulled the rear gunner from his turret and away from the flames. Despite suffering from severe burns, Thompson returned to his station. The Lancaster crash-landed near Brussels shortly thereafter and Thompson was rushed to hospital, where he died of pneumonia three weeks later – mid-upper gunner Sgt E. J. Potts also succumbed to his burns. Thompson, who was just 24 years of age, was awarded a posthumous Victoria Cross for his courage.

Amongst the first flak units to engage Allied heavy bombers were the guns of the Kriegsmarine, which had an extensive network of units situated along the Dutch, Belgium and French coasts. The most common gun used was the 105mm SKC C/32 on an MPL C/30 mount with a *Deckenschutzschild* armoured cupola, as seen here. These particular guns were sited at La Renardière, near Toulon, and were well known to heavy bomber crews of the Fifteenth Air Force. (NARA)

FLAK TACTICS

The *Flakwaffe*'s first line of defence was the numerous gun batteries located on the coast of the Netherlands and the Low Countries, with airspace over the former country being dubbed the 'bomber Autobahn'. Not wanting to miss an opportunity to take shots at Allied bombers as they approached and departed Germany, a flak belt was established along the Belgium and Dutch coast lines in 1942.

The *Flakwaffe* was also augmented by numerous batteries from the Kriegsmarine, whose units defended harbours and other naval assets. Often overlooked, these batteries were usually the first to engage bomber formations heading for targets in Germany. Eventually, 23 *Marine Flak* heavy batteries were deployed along the Dutch coast alone. For bomber crews about to head inland, the reception was always the same. According to Lancaster rear gunner WO Harry Irons of No. 9 Sqn, 'The flak on the Dutch coast was murderous – light flak from hundreds of guns. From a distance it looked like 20 fireworks nights all at once, with purples, blues, yellows – all different colours.'

As with their Allied counterparts, German flak gunners employed three methods of fire control against high-flying heavy bombers – continuously pointed fire, predicted concentration fire and barrage fire. Continuously pointed fire relied on good visual or gun-laying radar acquisition of the target formation. This type of fire was designed to place shells directly in front of the lead aircraft in the formation, the gunners expending a continuous pattern of bursts along the bombers' course. Each battery would maintain pointed fire until the formation was no longer in range, new batteries then taking over. It was the most accurate and dangerous form of heavy anti-aircraft fire used by the *Flakwaffe*.

Predicted concentration fire was less effective than continuously pointed fire. Used at night, through cloud cover or when radar information was of minimal quality, it needed the incoming formation to fly straight and level for about 90 seconds in order to achieve success. A master command post directed the fire of several batteries at once. With the bombers sighted, direction, angular height and altitude readings were taken at several points along the formation's incoming course. Based on these readings, an actual prediction was made as to where the formation would be in the sky prior to firing. Each battery was informed of this, and adjustments made so that the concentrated fire would strike the point of prediction at the given time. After the first rounds had been fired, a new prediction was calculated and a new concentration of shells salvoed.

The least effective method was barrage fire, which was used at night or when cloud prevented good visual aiming. It was designed to put as much flak as possible into a certain area of sky known as 'the box', which was usually located just outside the expected bomb release line of the incoming formation. If properly placed by the flak gunners, bomber crews had no choice but to fly through it.

Both RAF and USAAF crews would routinely experience all three types of flak during a typical frontline tour, with American heavy bombers being exposed to the more accurate continuously pointed fire due to its reliance on visual targeting methods. The introduction of gun-laying radar in 1942, however, greatly improved the *Flakwaffe*'s ability to hit bombers at night. Searchlight batteries also benefited.

No. 90 Sqn Lancaster I PD336, flown by unit CO and three-tour veteran Wg Cdr Peter Dunham, blows up in mid-air after suffering a direct hit by flak over Wesel on 19 February 1945 while still carrying its 10,000lb bomb load. Of the 168 Lancasters sent out that day, it was the only one lost. An explosion like this at night led many RAF bomber crews to believe the Germans were shooting up 'Scarecrow' rounds, designed to mimic an exploding aircraft. The Luftwaffe never had a shell large enough to produce such an effect, however. There is little doubt the 'Scarecrows' were, in fact, real bombers exploding. (Author's Collection)

Using radar targeting data, searchlight operators could now scour the night sky with a greater degree of certainty. Once caught in the beams, a bomber was tracked and visually fired upon. The Operational Research Section (ORS) of Bomber Command found that during a three-month period in 1942, searchlight-assisted flak batteries inflicted 70 per cent of all casualties experienced by RAF bombers. Another ORS study indicated that searchlights increased the number of bombers hit by flak by approximately 50 per cent. For British crews, the cover of darkness was no longer a blanket under which they could hide. Lancaster tail gunner WO Fred Vincent of No. 189 Sqn recalled:

Going into the target, you would become very apprehensive and nervous. The searchlights, flak, the fighters, the danger of collision, the danger of getting hit with your own bombs. If you had time to stop and think about being frightened, you weren't doing your job properly. At night, you could be flying for hours and hours in total darkness and then when you got over the target it was lighter than day because of the searchlights. All hell usually broke loose upon our arrival. The Germans knew that we dropped TIs [Target Indicators], which we all had to fly over at a designated height and time. The enemy knew this, so they just fired their flak through the bloody TIs.

In spite of a shortage of gun-laying radar sets for flak batteries at the start of 1942, RAF crews noticed a worrying improvement in gunners' accuracy even in poor weather. During an attack on Bremen on the night of 17 January 1942, crews reported moderate to intense heavy flak, accurately predicted through ten-tenths cloud cover'. It was also noted that German nightfighters had been recalled early that night due to bad weather and snow – conditions that had no impact on gun batteries. The response

For RAF bomber crews attacking an important German target, this was the pyrotechnic nightmare that usually 'greeted' them on their attack runs. Searchlights, bright target indicators, nightfighter flares, tracers, flaming aircraft, smoke and fire from the ground and bursting flak all contributed to the maelstrom. This photograph, taken by an RAF Film Production Unit Lancaster, clearly reveals the scene over Pforzheim on the night of 23/24 February 1945. A total of 367 Lancasters and 13 Mosquitoes took part, creating a firestorm that killed 17,600 people in the city. Bomber Command lost ten Lancasters over Germany to flak, with two more crashing in France. (Author's Collection)

to the Bremen raid clearly demonstrated that the Luftwaffe now had an all-weather guidance system in place for its flak batteries that allowed gunners to target British bombers through a full overcast via gun-laying radar. The latter would also come into its own when targeting American bombers performing 'blind-bombing' missions using H2X radar during daylight hours – the first such operation was undertaken on 3 November 1943.

Although the performance of gun-laying radar had clearly improved, these systems could still not attain the levels of accuracy associated with directed fire by optical or illuminated tracking. Facing a shortage of gun-laying radar throughout 1942, the *Flakwaffe* instructed German industry to develop an auxiliary firing control system known as the Malsi Converter. Col Norman E. Hartman of the US Army gave the following explanation of how the system worked in an article published in the November–December 1949 edition of the *Antiaircraft Journal*:

The Germans had developed a very useful piece of fire-control equipment called the "Malsi Converter". This device, in general, served the same purpose as the grid-plotting systems used in our [US] gun-battery command posts in the ETO. The functions of the "Malsi Converter" were:

a. To receive present position data from its radar and convert same to plots for the operations room.

b. To relocate present position data for use of an adjacent searchlight.

c. In event of failure of local radar, to accept data from a distant radar and relocate same for feeding into its own *Kommandogerät*.

d. In event of failure of its own *Kommandogerät*, to accept data from local radar and furnish firing data for the guns.

e. To quickly determine firing data for barrages when called for by the barrage officer in the operations room.

The use of the "Malsi Converter", therefore, provided good insurance against the loss of the firepower of normal methods of fire control. For example, with a *Grossbatterie* connected to two adjacent sites, it was possible for any one of the six available radars to supply firing data for all three *Grossbatterien*.

As a 16-year-old school boy, Jochen Mahncke remembers his time as a Mals Converter operator:

I was in high school in Berlin in 1943. At the beginning of the year, the headmaster of our school informed us that we were to be conscripted to serve in the city's anti-aircraft defences.

My early training consisted of drill marches and such, but because we were already Hitler Youth we knew the routine and moved on quickly. After a few weeks of training I was assigned to the 1st Battery of the 244th Heavy Flak Battalion [part of the 24th Flak

Two B-24Js from the 409th BS/93rd BG are met with a barrage of predicted fire while on their bomb runs as they approach a cloud-covered Augsburg on 1 March 1945. Radar-controlled, predicated fire was used when a solid overcast, as seen here, prevented gunners from relying on visual targeting methods. (NARA)

Regiment] with 12 88mm guns in the village of Seeburg, near west Berlin. Only the strong boys were assigned to work with the actual guns, as the shells were quite heavy. I was sent to man the underground command post. There, I worked with the *Flakumwertegerät* Malsi Converter. The Converter was a really big circular table with all sorts of measurements on it and a relief map of Berlin. During a raid, we would receive targeting data from the gun-laying radar and *Entfernungsmessgerät* [range finder]. We then converted that data into fire orders and sent it to the guns.

The British bombers flew at between 2,000–3,000m [6,500–9,800ft], a height they considered sufficient for accurate bombing at night. When the American Fortresses came a year later, they flew at heights of 8,000–10,000m [26,000–32,800ft] in order

The original armament of the massive flak towers was four single 105mm guns. Here, gunners prepare to fire from the Berlin 'Zoo Bunker'. While the *Flakwaffe* heavy guns had an average rate of fire of 15 rounds per minute, firing had to be suspended after 20–25 rounds to allow the barrel to cool down. Firing would usually recommence after five minutes. Barrel wear was also a problem. Because of the B-17's higher operational ceiling, the majority of flak batteries were stretched to the limit of their effective range. In 1944 the *Flakwaffe* lost 380 88mm flak guns per month due to excessive wear or destruction in combat. (Author's Collection)

to avoid the worst of the flak. During those raids we didn't fire. Our 88s didn't have the range, and only the 105mm guns in another battery would engage.

In the beginning we very much liked the army life, thanks to the uniforms and comradery. At first the people of Berlin laughed at us and called us 'little boys', but eventually the came to appreciate what we did and sent us cake and biscuits when they had any. In the beginning our teachers would visit us for lessons during the day, but as the bombing raids increased the tram and subway lines were no longer reliable. It was too far for them to walk so they simply stayed away. By the end of 1943 all school was over. I remember also being very tired. The pre-alarm of an incoming raid would sound at around 8pm, and wouldn't end until 4am the following morning. Fortunately, we didn't have to do any service work during the day.

I can't remember how many bombers we claimed as shot down. There were a few of course, and I believe we were reasonably effective. After one of the raids the NCO and I went on our bicycles to see if we could find any of the bombers claimed by our unit. We did find some aircraft, and, if I remember correctly, they were Lancasters.

Beginning in 1940, Luftwaffe construction teams went to great lengths to lure RAF bombers away from actual targets with decoy installations. In the early stages of the war they proved highly successful. These installations replicated factories, railway stations and other targets. Decoy sights were defended by 'barrier fire' batteries using captured enemy guns. These batteries, equipped with the most rudimentary optical range-finding devices and no gun-laying radar, provided a high volume of fire for a short period of time. Barrier fire batteries were also deployed to augment regular flak units in the defence of key sites.

With German cities being attacked by Bomber Command at night and American B-17s and B-24s undertaking daylight raids on industrial targets, the Luftwaffe knew it could not protect every important target in the Third Reich and the occupied territories. One response was to increase the number of heavy and light railway-based flak battalions. These mobile units became the flak elite, with the best equipment and best-trained crews. Able to move quickly, the units provided a robust defence for target areas that previously had few or no guns. They were also used to bolster existing defences around sites that faced constant attacks. By the end of 1943 there were 100 heavy and 20 light railway flak batteries in operation. The *Flakwaffe* also increased the number of guns per railway battery from four to six barrels, this being deemed to be the quickest way to add more firepower per individual battery.

To bring more concentrated fire to bear on daylight formations and the compact 'bomber streams' at night, *Großbatterien* (superbatteries) were formed. Each one consisted of three batteries of four guns linked to one centrally located gun-laying radar and three fire directors. Although this led to

A 128mm FlaK 40 railway gun sits ready for action. Due to its excessive weight, the 128mm weapon could only be employed statically or as a railway gun. Rail-based flak units were highly mobile, although by the end of 1943 their movement was largely dependent on the availability of coal for the locomotives that pulled them. (Author's Collection)

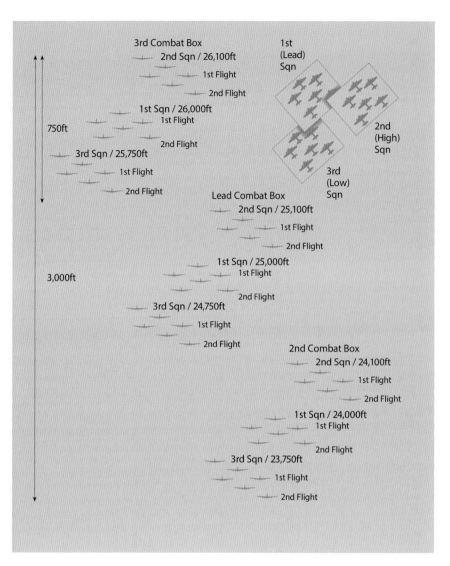

3rd Combat Box
2nd Sqn / 26,100ft
1st Flight
2nd Flight
1st Sqn / 26,000ft
1st Flight
2nd Flight
3rd Sqn / 25,750ft
1st Flight
2nd Flight

1st (Lead) Sqn
2nd (High) Sqn
3rd (Low) Sqn

750ft

3,000ft

Lead Combat Box
2nd Sqn / 25,100ft
1st Flight
2nd Flight
1st Sqn / 25,000ft
1st Flight
2nd Flight
3rd Sqn / 24,750ft
1st Flight
2nd Flight

2nd Combat Box
2nd Sqn / 24,100ft
1st Flight
2nd Flight
1st Sqn / 24,000ft
1st Flight
2nd Flight
3rd Sqn / 23,750ft
1st Flight
2nd Flight

The standard USAAF Combat Wing formation fielded 54 B-17s (sometimes mixed with B-24s) in three 'boxes' of bombers (in high, lead and low positions), each consisting of three six-aircraft squadrons that were also echeloned into lead, high and low positions. In turn, the squadrons were formed of two three-ship flights (high and low). Such a formation, despite requiring considerable time and disciplined flight control, ensured a high level of mutual protection and defence, although the bombers flying in the second flights of the low squadrons were most vulnerable to both flak and fighters.

fewer personnel being required to man the guns, superbatteries required well-trained crews to be effective.

ALLIED TACTICS

For Allied heavy bomber crews, flak was amongst the things they feared the most. Arriving unannounced, it was impersonal, dirty and, once on the bomb run (which could last up to two minutes), there was nothing you could do to avoid it. When under attack from enemy fighters, crews could at least shoot back, giving them a sense of control and a way to dispense their fear and anger. Inside a flak barrage, you were the target, as Fifteenth Air Force B-17 pilot 2Lt John Muirhead from the 32nd BS/301st BG explained in his autobiography, *Those Who Fall*:

When it came, it came like a mighty shout, a malediction hurling up at us through four miles of twisting wind. They were everywhere; the dark flowers of flak were everywhere. Four successive shells exploded in front of my right wing, and I felt the wheel tremble in my hands. An orange core glared out of a shroud of smoke in front of me. Our plane shuddered against the concussion of two bursts underneath us. My left wing dropped away from me, and I drove my foot hard against the right rudder to bring it up. I didn't pray, I didn't curse, I didn't think. I crouched in my cave of instruments, tubes and wires.

From the very beginning, Allied heavy bomber design focused on the concept of the 'self-defending bomber'. A great deal of expense and technology was devoted to achieving this. While heavy bombers bristled with powered turrets and machine guns, very little thought was given to the effects of flak on bombing accuracy and damage.

Early Allied tactics relied on speed and altitude through the target zone to avoid the worst of the flak. Having adopted the cover of darkness, Bomber Command believed that height was the best way to avoid casualties. Unfortunately for British crews, their heavy bombers were limited in their ability to reach higher altitudes. The mighty Lancaster was the best, but could only reach a ceiling of 24,000ft – well within the range of 88mm guns.

As losses to flak mounted, the idea of increasing the heavy bombers' speed was considered. During night operations it quickly became apparent that both the top and front turrets of the Stirling, Halifax and Lancaster were all but useless against German nightfighters, with the rear turret being not much better. The problem the heavy bombers had was that they were too slow and too heavily loaded. Operational research by distinguished British–American theoretical physicist and mathematician Freeman Dyson revealed that removing all the turrets from a Lancaster would increase its speed by as much as 50mph. Despite this finding, only the Halifax B III had the front turret removed. Although the extra speed might have made a huge difference to losses, 'Bomber' Harris believed the turrets had a 'good psychological effect on the crew'.

To counteract the increasing effectiveness of flak and nightfighters, the RAF introduced the 'bomber stream' in May 1942. As previously noted in this chapter, each aircraft would be allocated a height band and time slot over the target within the 'bomber stream'. A crew had to fly a steady course while on the bomb run and hope the searchlights and flak did not find them. Even as early as April 1942 it was evident that the increased flak and searchlight defences were adversely affecting aircrew in Bomber Command, as

The 150cm *Flakscheinwerfer 37* required a crew of 14 to operate it. Each four-gun battery commonly worked with a support unit equipped with nine 150cm searchlights. By June 1944 most searchlight units were operated by the women of the *Flak Kampfhelferinnen*. (Author's Collection)

RAF Scampton Station Commander Grp Capt Charles Whitworth (previously CO of Halifax-equipped No. 35 Sqn) noted at the time:

> There is no doubt about it – flak and searchlights frighten our people beyond measure and many crews go completely to pieces. I am of the opinion – and I happen to know what I am talking about – that in one average squadron today you will find only one out of five crews who are good enough and sufficiently brave enough to mix it with flak and searchlights in the Ruhr and bomb the target. The remainder just fling their bombs away in the area and are just 'fringe merchants'.

As one RAF veteran observed, 'fear was the eighth passenger in all heavy bombers'. Indeed, some crews and squadrons took the matter of survival into their own hands. To obtain greater height over the target, a number of Halifax squadrons reduced their bombloads by as much as a full ton. By 1944 the reports of 'fringe merchants' – crews who dropped their bombs early or released their heaviest bombs over the North Sea en route to the target – proliferated.

By then Bomber Command had introduced a number of measures aimed at defeating German gun-laying radar, with one of the most effective being codenamed *Window*. This had been driven by the results of a nine-raid offensive against the Ruhr in June 1943 that culminated with a massive attack on Cologne. The combined flak and nightfighter defences accounted for no fewer than 207 RAF bombers (nearly one-third of Bomber Command's frontline strength) during the offensive. While Harris was satisfied with the damage his crews had inflicted, it was clear that both German flak and nightfighters were gaining a decisive edge.

New tactics and countermeasures were needed, and on the night of 24–25 July 1943 Bomber Command used *Window* for the first time. The target was the city of Hamburg, which was attacked by 791 bombers (347 Lancasters, 246 Halifaxes, 125 Stirlings and 73 Wellingtons). *Window* (called chaff in the USAAF) consisted of 2,200 12-inch aluminum foil strips packed into a single bundle, with 12 bundles forming a *Window* parcel – a typical load for a Lancaster was 50 parcels. When 80 miles from the German coast, Pathfinders and main force bombers would drop their bundles of *Window*. The effect was devastating, blinding both ground-based *Würzburg* and nightfighter intercept radars. Flak gun-laying radar was also rendered useless, leaving searchlights to wander aimlessly and forcing flak batteries to employ barrier fire tactics. The Hamburg raid was a stunning success, with just four Lancasters, four Halifaxes, three Stirlings and one Wellington shot down.

Window's effectiveness did not last long, however. When used properly, it could effectively blind German radar in a given area, but high winds would scatter the strips, thus creating little in the way of radar interference. By the autumn of 1943 gun-laying radar operators had been issued with anti-jamming devices, thus restoring the effectiveness of the *Flakwaffe*.

One of the earliest tactics employed by Allied heavy bomber crews in their attempt to defeat German flak and increase accuracy was to attack at low-level, although it met with only limited success. On 17 April 1942, for example, 12 Lancasters (six each from Nos. 7 and 44 Sqns) mounted a low-level daylight raid on the MAN diesel engine factory at Augsburg, in Germany. Seven Lancasters were

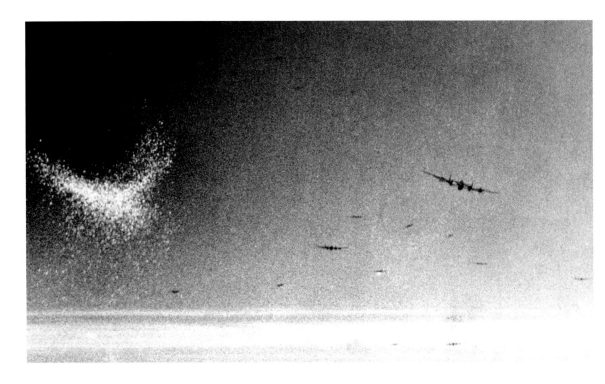

Once the RAF learned that German early warning radars operated on only four frequencies, their scientists were able to develop aluminium chaff strips known as *Window* to confuse enemy radars. Here, Lancasters drop clouds of *Window* over the Ruhr. Its introduction briefly switched the advantage to Bomber Command, and for a time Lancaster losses declined. (Imperial War Museum, C5635)

shot down, three of them falling to light flak. By the end of 1942 it was clear that undertaking low-level daylight missions in both heavy and medium bombers was extremely hazardous for the crews involved. An ORS report released in November 1942 recorded that between 1 July 1941 and 17 October 1942, the RAF lost 61 bombers and had a further 88 damaged during 403 low-level attacks. The creators of the document concluded that 'light flak at the targets is by far the most serious danger to be contended with on this type of operation'. Indeed, Luftwaffe light flak units accounted for 70 per cent of losses due to known causes during low-level missions.

Ignoring the British experience, the USAAF learned the hard way just how effective flak at low level really was when, on 1 August 1943, 176 B-24s mounted Operation *Tidal Wave* – a low-level attack on the Rumanian oil refineries at Ploesti. A navigational error on the run in gave the 15 heavy and 12 light batteries protecting the target ample warning of the approaching Liberators. Of the 166 B-24s that made it to the target, 33 were shot down by flak and ten by fighters, with a further 56 bombers damaged.

By late 1943 the USAAF began to take the science of 'flak analysis' seriously after it had realized, to its cost, that the *Flakwaffe* posed a far greater threat than had originally been estimated. The number of heavy bombers shot down and damaged was increasing month on month, forcing a change in tactics and the use of electronic countermeasures. In October of that year the USAAF introduced a gun-laying radar jammer codenamed *Carpet I*, and two months later, on 20 December, the Eighth Air Force used chaff for the first time. While these methods reduced losses, they were never totally effective.

In November 1944 Headquarters, Eighth Air Force Operational Analysis Section produced an in-depth study titled 'An Evaluation Taken to Protect Bombers from Loss and Damage'. The results were sobering. New tactics were recommended, but many of the old methods remained. The report read, in part, as follows:

During the past year enemy flak defenses have been concentrated and our bombers faced many more guns. The percentage of bombers lost to or damaged by enemy fighters has declined sharply, while the percentage lost to flak has declined only moderately. The percentage damaged by flak has remained almost constant. As a result, there has been a steady increase in the relative importance of flak until in June, July and August 1944, flak accounted for about two-thirds of the 700 bombers lost and 98 per cent of the 13,000 bombers damaged.

In number, the current rate is startling. From 3,360 to 4,453 bombers have returned with flak damage in each of the six months ending September 1944 – a monthly average just about double the total number damaged by flak in the entire first year of operations. All our efforts to reduce flak damage have apparently been offset by the fact that we have increasingly flown over targets defended by more and more guns. Further, enemy equipment, gunnery and ammunition have probably improved. The 60-gun target of a year ago is likely to be defended by 300 guns today. This makes it essential that we increase our efforts to decrease flak risks by re-examining the tactics we have been using and such new tactics as offer real possibilities.

The principal tactics to reduce flak risks are:

1. Avoid flying over flak defenses en route to and from the target

2. Enter and leave the target area on course, which cross over the weakest flak defenses in the shortest time possible – i.e. with allowances for wind vector.

3. Fly at the highest altitude consistent with other defensive and offensive considerations.

4. Plan the spacing and axes of attack of bombing units to make the fullest use of the radio countermeasures *Window* and *Carpet*.

5. Minimize the number of bombers flying together as a bombing unit.

6. Increase the spread of the entire formation in altitude and breadth to reduce the risk from barrage fire.

7. Close up in trail so as to reduce the time between attacks of successive bombing units, and thus saturate the enemy flak defenses when they are employing continuously pointed or predicted concentration firing tactics.

8. Plan evasive action when flying over known anti-aircraft positions (except on a bomb run) to make it difficult or impossible for the enemy to get accurate data for continuously pointed or predicted concentration firing tactics.

By January 1944, the Eighth and Fifteenth Air Forces could call upon an average of almost 3,000 heavy bombers for daily operations. Bomber Command added another 1,300–1,400 Lancaster and Halifaxes to that total. To meet the growing threat, the Luftwaffe's ground-based defences of the Reich and occupied territories reached a wartime high in February 1944 of 13,500 heavy guns, 21,000 light guns, 7,000 searchlights and 2,400 barrage balloons.

The 128mm Flakzwilling 40/2 was a massive weapon, weighing in at 28 tons. It also posed the greatest danger to high-flying bombers. In October 1944, a total of 102,450 128mm shells were fired at Allied heavy bombers – the most ever expended in a single month. (Author's Collection)

A veteran of 129 missions, B-17G 42-31333 *WEE WILLIE* of the 323rd BS/91st BG met its end over the German town of Kranenburg on 8 April 1945 when a direct flak hit between the fuselage and the No. 2 engine started a fierce fire. The latter eventually detached the bomber's port wing, as seen here. Of 42-31333's ten-man crew, only the pilot, 1Lt Robert E. Fuller, survived as a PoW. (NARA)

By the autumn of that year the combined Allied air forces (strategic and tactical) had complete air superiority over Germany and much of Europe. The absence of Luftwaffe fighters meant that the *Flakwaffe* stood alone in the defence of the crumbling Reich. By December, Germany lay open to devastating aerial bombardment.

Suffering from shortages of ammunition and the continued dilution of regular personnel with auxiliaries, foreign volunteers and PoWs, the *Flakwaffe* saw its accuracy and effectiveness deteriorate rapidly in the final months of the war in Europe. The massive transfer of flak batteries to join the ground battle in the East weakened the defences even further. During the first week of January 1945 the Luftwaffe transferred 110 heavy and 58 medium flak batteries eastward in a forlorn attempt to help slow the advance of the Soviet Red Army. Overall, in the last eight months of the war, the Luftwaffe transferred 555 heavy and 175 medium/light flak batteries to the fighting front. This massive transfer of guns and personnel effectively stripped entire cities in Germany of their defences. Even Berlin was not immune, losing 30 heavy and 13 light flak batteries and all of its searchlight crews, which were transferred to the infantry. These reinforcements did little to stem the Soviet invasion.

Yet despite the parlous situation it found itself in, the *Flakwaffe* continued to achieve good results in daylight visual conditions. This was confirmed in a monthly report submitted by the Eighth Air Force's 3rd Air Division, which confirmed that 'well-defended targets continue to put up effective flak when attacked under visual conditions'. Proof of this came on 3 February, when the Eighth Air Force despatched 1,003 bombers to attack Berlin. The weather was clear, and with no Luftwaffe fighters rising to challenge the bombers, flak batteries provided the capital with its only means of defence. Crews subsequently described the flak as 'murderous', with the guns shooting down 25 bombers and eight fighters, with a further 397 damaged (seven of the latter beyond repair).

The Allies rarely, if ever, directly targeted flak batteries. There were a few 'flak-busting' missions attempted by the RAF early in the war, with limited results. During the Hamburg raid in July 1943, Bomber Command dropped antipersonnel bombs on known gun sites, but this tactic was never repeated. It took the USAAF until April 1945 to target flak batteries with its heavy bombers, two trials being conducted by the Fifteenth Air Force on the 1st and the 19th, when B-24s dropped AN-M81 260lb fragmentation bombs near Grisolera, northeast of Venice in northern Italy. According to the official Fifteenth Air Force report, 'Bombers at high altitude can identify flak positions and drop 260lb fragmentation bombs with VT fuses accurately enough to cause diminution of accuracy and intensity of AA opposition. Bomber crews are very enthusiastic about anti-flak missions since they afforded an opportunity to fight back at the AA gunner.' Unfortunately for Allied heavy bomber crews, these tactics had not been adopted earlier.

STATISTICS AND ANALYSIS

'Increase in altitude, increase in the size of the attacking force and increase in the size of a [defensive] box decreased bombing accuracy.'
United States Strategic Bombing Survey

Since the end of World War II, flak's effectiveness has always been measured by the number of aircraft shot down. Often framed as less effective than fighters in this respect, flak was nevertheless responsible for destroying a significant number of Allied heavy bombers over occupied Europe. More importantly, however, flak caused thousands of bomber crews to miss their target – the very job it was designed for.

Evasive manoeuvring over the target due to flak significantly reduced 'accuracy' during both point target attacks and area bombing. Just how effective the *Flakwaffe* was at this is revealed in the statistics for the attacks on the Leuna synthetic oil refinery in early 1944. Surrounded by 500 heavy guns, including 150 prized 128mm

This 128mm FlaK 40 gun belonged to 14. *Flak Division*, which was charged with defending the Leuna synthetic oil refinery in central Germany. Although the best heavy anti-aircraft artillery weapon of the war, the FlaK 40 was only fielded in small numbers – just 1,125 FlaK 40s, including Flakzwilling 40/2s were built. Employed against approaching US Army forces in April 1945, the guns of 14. *Flak Division* claimed 147 American tanks destroyed during fighting in this sector. (Author's Collection)

Of all the Allied four-engined heavy bombers, the Short Stirling suffered the most from German flak defences. While capable of carrying a heavy bombload over a modest range, its low operating ceiling exposed it to both heavy and medium flak weapons. By mid-1941, Nos. 7 and 15 Sqns were equipped with Stirling Is, and during the summer and autumn of that year they mounted a number of increasingly hazardous daylight raids that quickly exposed the limitations of the Short heavy bomber. The month of July was one of the most intense, with Stirlings flying a succession of escorted daylight raids to targets in northern France. The number of aircraft involved in these operations was small (three to ten bombers) and the bombing results achieved were disappointing. Depending on the target, flak could be intense and effective. Over a two-week period from 5 to 19 July, three Stirlings were lost to flak defences alone as the German flak arm grew in strength to match the growing threat posed by Bomber Command.

weapons, Leuna would exact a heavy toll on Allied bombers. After several raids, the USAAF had lost 82 aircraft, with flak accounting for 59, fighters 13 and seven to accidents. After the war, the United States Strategic Bombing Survey found that heavy flak over Leuna 'undoubtedly contributed to inaccuracy in the bombing of the target'. The survey also found that just ten per cent of all bombs dropped fell within the target area – an expanse of 757 acres. When concentrated in very large numbers within a relatively small area, flak proved extremely effective, causing significant damage and, more importantly, decreasing accuracy.

In the wake of the disastrous 1 August 1943 attack on the heavily defended oil refineries at Ploesti, Fifteenth Air Force B-24s were forced to bomb this target from

24,000ft on subsequent raids. This attack profile usually required crews to jettison ordnance in order to reach such an altitude, and fewer bombs on target meant decreased accuracy. Post-war, USAAF studies revealed that 61.4 per cent of American radial bombing errors could be attributed to Luftwaffe flak. In Bomber Command, flak not only caused pilots to use evasive manoeuvres, but also contributed to the phenomenon known as 'creep back' – the tendency to bomb early.

In addition to decreasing bombing accuracy, aircraft damaged by flak often fell out of their protective formations. Without the supportive fire from other bombers, they became easy prey for Luftwaffe fighters. As one *Jagdflieger* recalled, 'That was the old fighter pilot's trick. The successful ones built up their scores in this way.'

It must also be remembered that USAAF bomber crews were forced to adopt British 'blinding-bombing' techniques from September 1943 because of persistent bad weather and cloud cover over Europe during autumn and winter. Using H2X ground-mapping radar and other radio navigational systems (specifically Bomber Command's *Oboe* and *Gee*), the USAAF was no longer performing precision attacks, but saturating entire areas with bombs, often with poor results. In the last quarter of 1944 close to 80 per cent of all Eighth Air Force missions used 'blind-bombing' devices.

In spite of increased Allied bombing from early 1944, the production of flak guns and equipment actually increased through to war's end. That year German industry produced 1,838 88mm (all types), 192 105mm, 202 128mm and an astounding 11,669 20mm guns.

The flak arm's effectiveness in the first quarter of 1944 also improved. In the first four months of that year, the Eighth and Fifteenth Air Forces lost 315 bombers to flak, with a further 10,563 damaged. Monthly reports from Eighth Air Force flak intelligence officers noted the improved performance of *Flakwaffe* batteries in the first quarter of 1944. In February, the flak intelligence officer for the 1st Bombardment Wing reported, 'Hun flak is improving slowly month by month, in spite of our chaff. If conclusions can be drawn from damage figures alone, then it might be claimed with reason that the use of chaff is a waste of time.' In April, the evidence was more startling. 'There is no doubt that the accuracy of flak has improved considerably during the last two months, in spite of the chaff that we drop, and in spite of all the various countermeasures.'

It was not until the autumn of 1944 that the effectiveness of the flak arm finally began to wane across Germany, as a result of serious ammunition shortages caused by constant Allied bombing.

Nevertheless, by VE Day, the *Flakwaffe* had more than proven its worth. Between July 1942 and April 1945 flak guns had shot down an estimated 1,345 Bomber Command aircraft during night sorties, while Luftwaffe nightfighters brought down an estimated 2,278 to give them a 1.69–to–1 advantage over the *Flakwaffe*. A further 2,072 aircraft were lost to 'unknown causes' and 112 'not by enemy aircraft'. No fewer than 8,842 bombers were damaged, 151 of them beyond repair, between February 1942 and April 1945. In total, the RAF lost 3,431 Lancasters, 1,884 Halifaxes and 625 Stirlings during day and night operations.

In comparison, the USAAF's Eighth and Fifteenth Air Forces would lose a little over half of its aircraft to flak – 5,400, compared to 4,300 shot down by Luftwaffe

fighters. The Eighth lost a total of 1,798 heavy bombers to flak, with the Fifteenth Air Force losing a further 1,046, between November 1943 and May 1945. In addition to the number of B-17s and B-24s the *Flakwaffe* shot down, and the effect it had on the bombing accuracy of American crews, German gunners damaged an astonishing 54,539 Eighth Air Force Flying Fortresses and Liberators between December 1942 and April 1945. The number of Fifteenth Air Force heavy bombers damaged by flak totalled 11,954.

A direct hit by a heavy flak shell was almost always fatal, although some aircraft such as B-17G 42-98004 of the 508th BS/351st BG had a lucky escape. During a raid on Cologne on 27 September 1944, an 88mm shell entered the fuselage near the rear entrance to the radio room and exploded, blasting away the ball turret with the gunner, Sgt Kenneth Divil, still inside – he was killed. Special radio operator Sgt John Kurtz, a German-speaker who was monitoring enemy transmissions for the Y Service, fell through the hole in the aircraft's fuselage but survived as a PoW. 42-98004 made it back to the 351st BG's Polebrook, Northamptonshire, base, where its pilot, Capt Jerome Geiger, was photographed surveying the damage prior to the aircraft being salvaged. (Author's Collection)

While many of these aircraft received only superficial damage and were quickly repaired, the number of 'seriously damaged' bombers was revealing. Between May 1944 and March 1945, the 1st Bombardment Wing listed 4,115 aircraft as seriously damaged from a total of 15,042 hit by flak. That meant slightly over 27 per cent of all aircraft hit by flak were seriously damaged. Assuming this number of seriously damaged bombers held across the command, the total number of B-17s and B-24s seriously damaged would have been an incredible 14,889 between December 1942 and March 1945. Furthermore, thousands of aircrew had been wounded, countless hours expended and precious resources used up returning non-operational aircraft to frontline service so as to maintain the round-the-clock bombing offensive against Germany.

Damaged bombers also sought the refuge of neutral countries like Sweden and Switzerland, with almost 200 crews having been interned by the end of 1944.

Although the often-quoted statistic that it took 16,000 88mm shells fired from a FlaK 36 or 37 gun to shoot down an Allied bomber is technically accurate, this has to be seen in context. The FlaK 36 and 37 were, by some margin, the most common flak guns fielded by the Germans. With an effective range of up to 26,000ft, 88mm flak batteries were hard pressed to engage higher-flying B-17s, which normally overflew their targets at between 24,000–26,000ft. Add excessive barrel wear (many guns were used well beyond their normal operational lives), a lack of sophisticated fire control equipment for *Flak Wehrmanner* units, the influx of poorly trained auxiliaries in 1943–44 and Allied radar countermeasures, and it quickly becomes obvious why it typically took 16,000 88mm rounds to down a single bomber. By comparison, 'elite' crews who manned the superior 128mm FlaK 40 gun averaged just 3,000 rounds per victory.

What has never been calculated was how many rounds it took to cause a bomber crew to miss their target? Had the Germans developed their own 'proximity-fused' flak shell in 1943, the results would have been disastrous for the Allies.

During the war, estimates of rounds expended per aircraft destroyed averaged between 2,805 and 4,000 rounds of heavy flak ammunition. Averaging it out to 3,400 rounds per victory, the cost of manufacturing the shells required to bring down a heavy bomber totalled 267,440 Reichmarks or US$106,976. The cost of a fully equipped B-17 was approximately US$292,000, the B-24 totalled US$327,000 and the Lancaster £320,000. These figures do not take into account the cost accrued in the manning of either bombers or flak batteries, or the development and construction of specialized equipment required for these weapon systems. In a straight comparison, the cost of US$107,000 per victory for the heavy flak guns was a more than fair return. Add in the cost of repair for the thousands of damaged bombers and aircraft that returned to base but had to be scrapped and the ratio increases still further in the flak gun's favour.

The exchange in blood also favoured the flak batteries. While tens of thousands of highly trained Allied aircrew perished or were wounded by flak, the *Flakwaffe* suffered minimal casualties during air raids. In the war of attrition, the heavy flak gun proved a lethal adversary.

During World War II, British and American heavy bombers expended 1.2 million tons of bombs on targets in Germany. An estimated 300,000 German civilians were killed, 780,000 wounded and 3.6 million dwellings destroyed. In return, Bomber Command would have 47,286 aircrew killed. Eighth Air Force heavy bomber casualties numbered more than 47,000, with 26,000 aircrew killed. The Fifteenth Air Force would have 20,430 bomber crewmen killed, wounded or captured.

A waist gunner's view of heavy flak exploding around 457th BG B-17s over Schweinfurt on 24 February 1944. Bombing was carried out through a heavy overcast that day and 11 Flying Fortresses were lost during the mission. Bomber Command followed up with an attack during the night of 24/25 February, losing 26 Lancasters and seven Halifaxes to flak and nightfighters. (Author's Collection)

AFTERMATH

'We never conquered the German flak artillery.'
Gen Henry H. 'Hap' Arnold

Like a medieval castle, the 'Holy Ghost' flak tower in Hamburg stands as a mute testament to the considerable resources allocated to the *Flakwaffe* by Hitler during the war. These huge structures (also found in Berlin and Vienna) were in fact air raid shelters with flak batteries on top of them. (Author's Collection)

Before and during the war, both the RAF and USAAF underestimated the overall effect that flak could have on bombing accuracy, as well as its ability to shoot aircraft down. Conversely, it is also true that Hitler and Göring overestimated its effectiveness, with the former giving priority to the *Flakwaffe* as Germany's main method of defence against the heavy bomber.

By the autumn of 1944, Allied air superiority over Germany was complete, leaving the defence of the airspace over the Third Reich largely to ground-based flak batteries and searchlights. That year, flak defences in Germany and the occupied territories accounted for the destruction of 6,385 aircraft, with a further 27,000 damaged. For Allied heavy bomber crews, flak would be a deadly constant right up to the very end of the war. On 25 April 1945, the Eighth Air Force launched its last heavy bomber raid, involving 307 B-17s and 288 B-24s. While flak failed to shoot any of the bombers down, 200 were damaged – four of these were listed as 'category E', which meant that they were beyond repair.

The Allied strategic bombing campaign against Germany was not as decisive as had been hoped for. The belief that 'an attack on the economic heart of the enemy's country would result in a quick and relatively bloodless victory' turned into a long, bloody battle of attrition. Without a doubt, flak batteries played an integral role in the air defence of Germany, and helped maintain its war fighting ability well into 1944. Indeed, war production increased that year, with more tanks and fighters being built in 1944 than in 1943 (10,000 fighters were delivered in 1943 and more than 20,000 in 1944). However, while these numbers may have been impressive, the machines were all but useless without fuel or able-bodied men to operate them. War on three fronts had all but exhausted Germany's manpower reserves, and its ability to produce the fuel, oil and lubricants needed to keep its aircraft flying had been drastically affected by Allied bombing.

Germany's heavy flak defences have often been dismissed as wasteful (both in terms of manpower allocated to the *Flakwaffe* and the ammunition it expended), with historians stating that the men and guns could have been used more effectively on the Eastern Front or against the Allies in the wake of the D-Day landings. In the autumn of 1944, the *Flakwaffe* was assigned 1,110,900 personnel – a formidable number by any measure. A closer look reveals that 448,700 of that number, or 40 per cent, were non-Luftwaffe personnel consisting of 220,000 Home Guard, Labor Service and high school boys, 128,000 female auxiliaries and 98,000 foreign volunteers and PoWs. Of the regular Luftwaffe service personnel, 21 per cent were between the ages of 39 and 48 and 35 per cent were older, or had been declared medically unfit for frontline duty.

An abandoned 88mm gun, its muzzle marked with at least 16 victory bands, points skyward in front of the heavily damaged Reichstag in Berlin in late 1945. In the end, the Luftwaffe's ground-based defences could not prevent Allied heavy bombers from sowing destruction across Germany. (Author's Collection)

It must also be remembered that the *Flakwaffe* increasingly fought on two fronts, with a large proportion of the active Luftwaffe-manned flak units being assigned to ground combat on all fronts in the final months of the war. Shortly after D-Day, the Luftwaffe transferred 140 heavy and 50 light flak batteries to France. For the Wehrmacht, the *Flakwaffe* acted as the last, best reserve of guns and capable crews. From August 1944 the transfer of flak forces from German cities to the frontlines became common practice, robbing the home front of adequate ground defences.

In the end, the Luftwaffe's flak forces took a heavy toll of both Allied aircraft and armour. While they added to the Wehrmacht's fighting ability, they were outnumbered and finally overwhelmed. Losses in equipment and men on all fronts were heavy, with no chance of replacement. During the Battle of the Bulge in December 1944, for example, the *Flakwaffe* sacrificed 100 heavy and 110 light flak batteries for no real gain.

For the heavy bomber crews flying over Germany, flak exacted a heavy toll on them. While the ground-based defences alone could not stop the onslaught, without them, German cities and industry would have been bombed into ruin far sooner.

FURTHER READING

BOOKS

Bowman, Martin W., *USAAF Handbook 1939–1945* (Stackpole Books, Mechanicsburg, 1997)

Budiansky, Stephen, *Air Power* (The Penguin Group, New York, 2004)

Carter, William and Dunmore, Spencer, *Reap the Whirlwind – The Untold Story of 6 Group, Canada's Bomber Force of World War II* (McClelland and Stewart Inc., Toronto, 1991)

Copp, Terry, *Montgomery's Scientists Operational Research in Northwest Europe* (Wilfred Laurier University, Waterloo, 2000)

Falconer, Jonathan, *Osprey Combat Aircraft 124 – Short Stirling Units of World War 2* (Osprey Publishing, Oxford, 2018)

Forczyk, Robert, *Osprey Duel 51 – Bf 110 vs Lancaster 1942–45* (Osprey Publishing, Oxford, 2013)

Freeman, Roger A., *The Mighty Eighth – Units, Men and Machines: A History of the US Eighth Army Air Force* (MacDonald & Co., London, 1970)

Freeman, Roger A., *B-17 Flying Fortress at War* (Charles Scribner & Sons, New York, 1977)

Freeman, Roger A., *Mighty Eighth War Manual* (Jane's, London, 1984)

Freeman, Roger A., *Mighty Eighth War Diary* (Jane's, London, 1984)

Greenhouse, Brereton, Harris, Stephen J., Johnston, William C. and Rawling, William G. P., *The Crucible of War 1939–1945 – The Official History of the Royal Canadian Air Force Volume III* (University of Toronto Press Inc., Toronto, 1994

Hogg, Ian V., *The Guns 1939–45* (Ballantine Books Inc., New York, 1970)

Hogg, Ian V., *Anti-Aircraft – A History of Air Defence* (Macdonald and Jane's Publishers Lt d, London, 1978)

Jarrett, Philip, *Aircraft of the Second World War* (Putnam Aeronautical Books, London, 1997)

Kaplan, Philip and Currie, Jack, *Round the Clock* (Random House Inc., New York, 1993)

Lake, Jon, *Osprey Combat Aircraft 14 – Halifax Squadrons of World War 2* (Osprey Publishing, Oxford, 1999)

March, Daniel, J., *British Warplanes of World War II* (Aerospace Publishing Lt d, London, 1998)

Middlebrook, Martin and Everitt, Chris, *The Bomber Command War Diaries* (Penguin Books, London, 1990)

Murray, Williamson, *The Luftwaffe 1933-45 – Strategy for Defeat* (Brassey's, Washington, D.C., 1989)

Nijboer, Donald, *Graphic War – The Secret Aviation Drawings and Illustrations of World War II* (Boston Mills Press, Erin, 2005)

Norris, John, *Osprey New Vanguard 46 – 88 mm Flak 18/36/37/41 & PaK 43 1936-45* (Osprey Publishing, Oxford, 2002)

Price, Alfred, *The Luftwaffe Data Book* (Greenhill Books/Stackpole Books, London, 1997)

Price, Alfred, *Luftwaffe Handbook* (Charles Scribner & Sons, New York, 1977)

Westermann, Edward B., *Flak – German Anti-Aircraft Defenses 1914–1945* (University Press of Kansas, Lawrence, 2001)

Zaloga, Steven J., *Osprey Fortress 102 – Defense of the Rhine 1944–45* (Osprey Publishing, Oxford, 2011)

Zaloga, Steven J., *Osprey Fortress 107 – Defense of the Third Reich* (Osprey Publishing, Oxford, 2012)

Zaloga, Steven J., *Osprey Campaign 236 – Operation Point Blank 1944* (Osprey Publishing, Oxford, 2011)

DOCUMENTS

The Strategic Air War Against Germany 1939–45 – British Bombing Survey (undated)

Flak Facts: A brief History of Flak and Flak Intelligence in the Ninth Air Force – Headquarters, Ninth Air Force, Flak Section, 1945

An Evaluation of Defense Measures Taken to Protect Heavy Bombers from Loss and Damage – Headquarters, Eighth Air Force Operational Analysis Section, November 1944

Anti-Aircraft Artillery Notes No. 8 – Headquarters, European Theatre of Operations, 13 December 1944

Light, Intense and Accurate, US Eighth Air Force Strategic Fighters versus German Flak in the ETO, 1943–1945 – Headquarters, Eighth Air Force Operational Analysis Section (undated)

Flak Facts, A Brief History of Flak and Flak Intelligence in the Ninth Air Force – APO 696 US Army (undated)

WEBSITES

www.ibiblio.org
www.jaegerplatoon.net
www.8thafhs.org
www.aircrewremembered.com

INDEX

References to images are in **bold**.